# Modern Rock Climbing
## *Free climbing and training beyond the basics*

# Modern Rock Climbing
## Free climbing and training beyond the basics

## by Todd Skinner
### and John McMullen

*Illustrations by John McMullen*

ICS BOOKS, Inc.
Merrillville, Indiana

## MODERN ROCK CLIMBING

### Printed in U.S.A.

All ICS titles are printed on 50% recycled paper for pre-consumer waste. All sheets are processed without using acid.

**PUBLISHER'S NOTE**

The sport described in this book can be inherently dangerous, and any person, especially inexperienced, undertaking it should approach it with extreme caution and appropriate supervision. The publisher cannot accept responsibility for any accidents, injuries, or losses suffered by any reader of this book however they may be caused. This book is not a substitute for professional instruction. It is the publisher's recommendation that individuals seek out instructional courses to increase safety to each participant. It is recommended to see a physician for a complete physical before starting any outdoor activity listed in this book.

**Published by:**
ICS Books, Inc.
1370 E. 86th Place
Merrillville, IN 46410
800-541-7323

**Library of Congress Cataloging-in-Publication Data**

Skinner, Todd, 1958–
    Modern rock climbing : beyond the basics / by Todd Skinner and John McMullen.
        p. cm.
    Includes index.
    ISBN 0-934802-90-4
    1. Rock climbing.  I. Skinner, Todd.  II. Title.
GV200.2.M37 1993
796.5'223—dc20                                    92-47396
                                                  CIP

# DEDICATION

This book is dedicated to all young climbers who with excitement and enthusiasm have found themselves starting a lifelong pursuit involving adventure and creativity, as well as danger. PLEASE! Be careful out there.

I would like to thank the following people for their help, information, motivation, and assistance. Mr. and Mrs. Vernon Lagamann, Catherine Carlisle-McMullen, Brents & Arcy at the Teton Rock Gym, Dave Berkenfield, Sean Sullivan, and the others at the gym, Karen Piel at 5.10, as well as the Lander bunch of Amy Whisler, Jacob Valdez, and other Cowboyography partners. Thanks to Galen Rowell and Bill Hatcher for the excellent Photographs.

And special thanks to Thomas Todd our publisher (you can put down the whip now, Tom). Without his help and patience, this book would still be at the tying-in stage.

We would also like to dedicate this book to the Wyoming cowboy who still wanders amid some of the finest crags in the world.

# TABLE OF CONTENTS

# ILLUSTRATIONS

# Appendix A

# Photographs

# FOREWORD

Welcome to the sport of rock climbing! No sport is wilder, more addictive, or more likely to take you to the strange corners of this planet. At its best, climbing becomes a life focus around which everything else must orbit and at its least is an excellent diversion from the real world. This is a sport that can be enjoyed by men and women equally, by nine-year-olds and ninety-year-olds, by dabblers and fanatics. No stretch of rock is like another, and a lifetime is not enough to climb everything in Wyoming much less the rest of America. You make up the rules for your vision, and you climb for as long as you are hungry to climb. There are no coaches, and there is no finish line. You are as good as you can be, or you are not—all that you throw into the rock comes back into yourself. We become the result of our struggles, the sum of our efforts. Stay true to yourself, speak badly of no one, and don't let the wind blow your hat off!

*Todd Skinner*

# INTRODUCTION

In 1974, I bought a copy of Doug Scott's book *Big Wall Climbing*. In the introduction he discussed the seven categories of climbing, a concept originated by mountaineer and philosopher Lito Tejada-Flores. Lito said that climbing is separated into a number of games the climber can play. As a youngster, I perceived this list as progressive, one game leading to the next. At the time, my only interest was to become a great alpine climber. So I worked toward that goal.

I learned the technical skills that would lead to ascents of the big walls. At first I practiced every technique I could on the small limestone cliffs that surrounded my home, in of all places, Missouri. I studied every piece of climbing literature I could get my hands on and fanatically memorized every piece of work I read. I lived the climbing lifestyle in Colorado, Southern California, and Arizona, and now live in majestic Grand Teton National Park: all in an effort to learn as much as possible about climbing. I spent many years "Paying my dues," and eventually graduated to the big walls, ice climbs, and alpine peaks of my dreams.

Little did I know at the time that I would end up enjoying crag climbing more than any other form of the game. Over the last twenty years, I have tried many of the games climbers play and always come back to the challenge of the "small walls," that challenge being focused on power and difficulty.

Now that the "modern" age of climbing is upon us, I for one embrace it—enjoying every new climb and the challenge of the future. Climbing has changed so much since I bought my first rope in 1972. There are now more climbers than ever, and they are improving at an incredible rate. I feel they are a healthy group, motivated by desire for power and pureness of thought. It is critically important that they learn the full spectrum of climbing skills, the most important being safety.

My main reason for writing this book is to create interest. Interest not only in the act of climbing but in the knowledge required to make the sport as safe as possible. To the many climbers out there who need technical information on technique and the use of modern climbing equipment, I hope this book will aid you.

With the help of one of the country's leading free and adventure climbers, Todd Skinner, I hope I can lead you in the right direction and give you an idea of what's happening out on the rock as well as in the gym.

It is difficult to give climbing instruction through a book. I advise that you take the information in this book and put it to practice on rock. Get help from an experienced climber, or get instruction from a qualified guide service. Learning to climb is a skill that can only be attained through practice. I can give you only raw data; it is up to you to go out and learn how to use it.

When I first envisioned writing this book, I never thought I would get the kind of support I have been given. At this time I would like to give my publisher, Tom Todd, a special thank you. Without his positive attitude and excitement about climbing, this book would not have been possible.

*John J. McMullen*

# 1. Modern Rock Climbing

All that is not given is lost.

*— Hasan Pal*

To define modern rock climbing is both easy and impossible. If you look at all the people who climb and call them a group, then what the majority of that group is doing is modern rock climbing. By this mainstream affiliation, the definition of "modern" will lean toward bolt-protected face climbing. If you look at all the people who climb and call them individuals, then what each climber is doing is modern rock climbing. One million climbers practice one million versions of the activity. We will largely use the first definition of modern rock climbing, while recognizing the second as an example of the freedom that makes climbing so diverse and appealing.

## The Basics of Technical Rock Climbing

Rock climbing is becoming a specialized sport. Crag climbing is no longer necessarily a method of training for the big walls or for the great epics in mountaineering. Rock climbing is a valid pursuit of its own. Some of the most difficult and most popular climbs in the world are less than forty feet long. And climbers now often focus their energies only on pure power, almost with the intensity of Olympic athletics.

1

Figure 1-1

Rock climbing involves several basic methods. Two are: *free climbing* and *aid climbing.*

A free climber depends entirely upon his footwork, ability, skill, and physical strength to pull himself up the rock face. The equipment used while free climbing is essentially for safety, i.e., protection to stop a fall. Equipment is not used to ascend the face directly. If you were to place a piece of protection in a crack and hang on it, or use it to reach a higher hold, you would not be free climbing in the "pure" sense of the word.

Any use of equipment to directly ascend a rock face is called aid. Aid techniques are used when a section of rock cannot be free climbed and equipment must be used to make progress up the rock.

Many modern free climbs involve the use of aid and free climbing techniques combined. The methods used to preplace bolts and other protection and the process of practicing moves are closely related to traditional aid climbing. Basic free climbing techniques are the foundation for advanced modern climbing. It is important to be proficient in the use of equipment and free climbing skill to be successful on today's modern rock climbs.

## A Little History-What is Traditional Climbing?

Rock climbing has been around for a long time, and the activity has only recently been described as a "sport." Past and pioneer climbers were interested above all in the adventure of climbing or the art and spirituality of it and did not consider their activity as sport. Would an astronaut consider a mission to the moon sport? Seriously, mountaineering, like space travel, is an adventure of the greatest magnitude. The mountaineer's competition is within himself and against the elements. His objective: to reach the summit and return alive.

### *Pushing the Envelope*

Pure difficulty became the objective of those with a more localized focus. Nationalism spurred competitiveness as countries subtly pitted themselves against one another in an attempt to reach the ultimate level of difficulty in the mountains. The glory won by success fueled the competition. Climbers have always tried to outdo each other, usually in a friendly way.

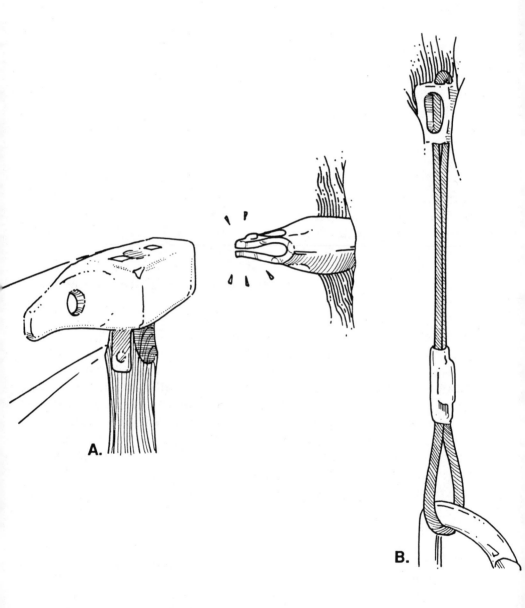

**Figure 1-2** A. Piton placements can damage the rock. B. Clean protection is easily
placed and doesn't damage the rock.

### Climbing Styles

Free climbing is a more natural style of climbing, less dependent upon equipment and technology. In the early days, climbers resorted to the use of equipment only if they could not advance beyond a "hard" move. The equipment used was so primitive that its lack or its ineffectiveness often caused failure (retreat) more so than did the weaknesses of the climber. The spirit and/or art of the climber had to rise to the surface as the decisive factor in success.

With the invention of the p*iton*, aid climbing became an acceptable method to achieve the summit. For a short time, pitons were the primary tools for climbing and allowed skillful climbers to ascend any piece of rock that had even the smallest crack in it.

Sometime in the mid-1960's, climbers in America began to realize that repeated ascents of routes using pitons were causing obvious permanent damage to the rock. Something had to be done. Enter the "clean climbing age." Following the example of the British, America's Royal Robbins and climbers around the world began slinging *machine nuts*. These crude slung nuts were slotted into constrictions in cracks, offering a "clean" alternative to the use of pitons.

A few climbers manufactured nuts that were specifically designed for climbing. American climbers Tom Frost and Yvon Chouinard designed some of the best. Their Stoppers and Hexentrics greatly contributed to the possibilities for clean climbing. In fact, nuts were easier than pitons. They were more creative but took less physical effort to place and remove. The introduction of clean climbing gear thus accelerated the free climbing movement, and climbers continued to push their limits but with a greater ecological sensitivity.

Climbers were challenged to free many of the routes that had previously only been climbed using aid climbing techniques. A strong new breed of free climber was being created. This continued for a number of years, and just when climbers thought they had reached their limit a new clean climbing device appeared on the scene: the *spring-loaded camming device* or *SLCD*.

The first commercially available SLCD was the Wild Country "Friend." SLCDs enabled the climber to place protection in perfectly parallel cracks with little or no effort, opening up a

**Figure 1-3**  Bolts placed traditionally often produced "runouts."

multitude of possibilities. All types of crack climbs could be done faster and with a high level of safety. The level of difficulty that could be achieved climbing with Friends certainly pushed the grade scale of crack climbing higher. Modifications on the camming device soon showed up. Three cam units, or TCUs, were smaller versions of the Friend and allowed for placements in cracks down to three quarters of an inch wide.

### *The Introduction of Modern Face Climbing*
To this time, the methods used to put up new routes were primarily traditional. That is, they were established from the ground up. Climbers didn't feel it was ethical to go to the top by an easy route and then rappel down to preview the route or pre-place protection. They started from the ground on even the smallest crags. The "ground-up" method was the goal most climbers shared at that time. In this way, the non-specialists trained for bigger climbs they hoped to do in Yosemite, the Alps, or Himalayas. These objectives, after all, would definitely have to be tackled from the ground.

The traditional method required that the natural features of the rock, or "cracks," be used for protection. Permanent anchors were used only if no other forms of security were available and where no cracks existed. Crackless face climbing, placing occasional bolts on the lead, was most beautifully illustrated on the domes of Tuolumne, above Yosemite. Using tiny quarter-inch bolts, climbers placed permanent anchors in the rock faces-allowing them to free climb with at least minimal protection. Being the bold climbers they were, they often refused to place the protection frequently. They climbed the routes with the fewest bolts possible-creating routes that required boldness and ambition but that were not always safe. The runout, they felt, made the placement of permanent protection ethical, since the bolts were not actually taking away from the sense of adventure. Certainly this style did not reduce the climbs to the level of the first ascentionists but tried rather to avoid a conveniently bolted line and tried to preserve some fear factor.

During the early 1980's in France, a small group of climbers began combining free and aid methods in order to "work" routes that were new and extremely difficult. They used the rope and equipment to support and aid themselves until they could climb the route not using the aid.

The routes were pre-protected by permanent anchors (bolts) placed so that any serious fall could be avoided. Preplaced protection provided security, allowing climbers to concentrate only on the difficulties involved in climbing and not the danger. This method proved to be beneficial in developing advanced technique and enabled those climbers using it to improve at an incredible rate.

In 1985, two French climbers who had adopted this new style visited Great Britain and impressively climbed many of the hardest routes. After practicing it, one of them free soloed the hardest route in the country. Climbers around the world looked on as France began to produce many of the best climbers in the world. It didn't take long for other climbers to adopt the techniques developed in France, and soon climbers throughout the world were improving as well.

At this time there was a separation in the climbing world. Traditionalists believed that the ultimate style and difficulty lay in the use of less equipment or none. A new group of climbers was forming who believed the ultimate could only be achieved if the danger was decreased, or in effect eliminated, while they improved technique and increased their strength. Many did not and still do not know that this battle of ethics had been going on since the first climber placed a piton in the rock.

## Modern Techniques

Many modern routes require the placement of clean climbing gear. The invention of the spring-loaded camming device and "Lowe/Byrne" ball nuts have opened new possibilities in the area of clean ascents. However, the level of difficulty attainable using and placing this equipment *while* climbing has not even come close to the level reached by the modern face climber. Climbers attempting to push the limits of clean climbing must often place their gear in the cracks prior to climbing a route of extreme difficulty. It is often difficult to set such protection while executing moves at this level.

Although this style of climbing is tough to learn and requires years of patient practice, climbs achieved using traditional methods carry a high level of satisfaction when completed and should by no means be written off as passé. There are hundreds, if not thousands of climbs, waiting to be done using these traditional tools.

Many of the skills learned through traditional climbing will greatly improve your ability as a modern climber.

### *Establishing a Modern Route*

A modern free climb may be established in any number of ways, not excluding the traditional method. A route may be established from the ground up or from the top down. By top down, we mean that protection can be placed before an attempt on the route. This includes clean climbing gear if it can be placed, or permanent anchors if the situation calls for such. The goal of the modern free climber is to climb at the highest level of one's ability without falling. It is allowable to rehearse the climb before an ascent, although this admittedly lowers the level of style in which the ascent is made. Modern rock climbing is more than a combination of all that we have learned in the past. It is the further development of that knowledge, meshed with new technique, as occurs in gymnastics.

## Coexisting Ethics and the Preservation of Access

Climbers live a lifestyle of freedom. We travel from place to place looking for new adventures and challenges. In the past, it seemed that climbers searched for a common goal, but this is now less so. Some look to the mountains, others are satisfied with small cliffs and the challenge of gymnastic difficulty. We are all individuals trying to express our individuality in climbing. But our resource of rock is not infinite. We must take care that we do not destroy our climbing areas, thereby risking their closure by private, federal, or state agencies.

Some things you can do to help open an area to climbing or keep existing areas open:

- Attempt to communicate in a caring spirit with the local population or agencies involved. Work toward establishing a healthy relationship with these people and the climbing community.
- Help keep your climbing areas clean. Make it a habit to pick up not only your trash, but assist the other users of the area by picking up any trash that you can. Don't allow other climbers to trash out your climbing area.

| USA | French | Australian/ South African |
|---|---|---|
| 5.4 | | 10 |
| 5.5 | | |
| 5.6 | | 12 |
| 5.7 | 5a | 14 |
| 5.8 | 5b | 16 |
| 5.9 | 5c | 18 |
| 5.10a | | 20 |
| 5.10b | 6a | 21 |
| 5.10c | 6a+ | 22 |
| 5.10d | 6b | |
| 5.11a | 6a+ | 23 |
| 5.11b | 6c | 24 |
| 5.11c | 6c+ | |
| 5.11d | 7a | 25 |
| 5.12a | 7a+ | |
| 5.12b | 7b | 26 |
| 5.12c | 7b+ | 27 |
| 5.12d | 7c | 28 |
| 5.13a | 7c+ | 29 |
| 5.13b | 8a | 30 |
| 5.13c | 8a+ | 31 |
| 5.13d | 8b | |
| 5.14a | 8b+ | 32 |
| 5.14b | 8c | 33 |
| 5.14c | 8c+ | 34 |
| 5.14d | 9a | |
| 5.15a | 9a+ | |

Figure 1-4

- Areas that are open to bolting still require that you do not mark or damage the rock. Do not vandalize, create graffiti, or leave ugly and obscene marks.
- Stay on established trails when possible. Do not create shortcuts that may cause erosion or trail damage. These paths take many hours to construct. Their creators should be rewarded; however, they seldom are.

Climbers of both factions should spend time looking at the problems that exist in their local climbing areas and learn to communicate with each other. This is the only way we will all be happy. That's why we climb isn't it?

## Rating Rock Climbs

The modern rating systems have enlarged considerably over the last ten years, and even more so over the last twenty. The hardest free climbs in the United States in 1963 were rated 5.10, and there were not many of them. As of this writing, the hardest climb in the United States is rated 5.14c. The hardest in the world may be 5.15! Modern free climbing has become an established sport with seemingly limitless boundaries. But as climbers struggle to improve, they raise standards of difficulty to impressive levels. Figure 1-4 shows several rating systems and their relationship to each other.

The primary purpose of rating a climb is to inform other climbers of the difficulties they may encounter. Ratings are a subjective form of reference. They should be taken as such. In the United States, you will find that a climb that is considered risky may have a rating followed by an R (for runout) or an X (meaning no protection is available, natural or otherwise). Such unprotected climbs are less frequent, but they exist.

While traditional climbers have played an important part in the evolution of the rating scale, and have achieved the boldest climbs, the modern free climber has achieved climbs that are more gymnastically difficult than those achieved using traditional methods. The use of permanent anchors on some modern routes allows climbers to concentrate on the difficulty of a climb rather than the danger. This does not mean that there are no risks involved in this type of climbing; there are, and we will address those dangers.

It's not that I'm afraid to die. I just don't want to be
there when it happens.

*—Woody Allen*

## Sport Climbing Competitions

During the 1980's, equipment manufacturers and climbing
promoters began sponsoring competitive climbing events in
Europe. Climbing competitions draw some of the outstanding
climbers from around the world to compete head to head with
each other. This is competition climbing (or sometimes referred
to only as sport climbing). With the incentive of money and
fame, climbers compete in a variety of events-such as on-sight
climbing and redpoint climbing.

Competition climbing has brought a creative new alternative
to climbers and certainly has "professionalized" the sport. A
climber who commits to the professional lifestyle is often able
to acquire sponsorship, enabling him or her to travel and climb
while making a somewhat modest living. Professional climbers
are often involved in workshops and various other services for
their sponsors while at the same time traveling to different
climbing areas. Becoming a pro requires a serious commitment
to the sport. The hard work of training and the pressures
related to competition are rewarded not only in cash but in the
availability of travel to national and international competitions
and foreign climbing areas.

## The Impact of Sport Climbing

There are many positive aspects to sport climbing, but I feel
it is necessary to reflect on a few of the negative consequences.
While the introduction of bolt-protected climbs has opened the
doors to more difficult climbing for the expert, they have also
created a hazard that is easily accessible to the novice.

Many young climbers are learning to climb in a new way;
that is, with a minimal amount of equipment and with a
minimal amount of knowledge of the dangers involved in the
use of that equipment. Climbers who learn to climb in a rock
gym are often confused when they are faced with real rock,
because they have not learned the use of all the equipment.
There are many aspects of climbing that are not possible to
teach in a gym that are very important to learn if you are going

to climb outdoors. And gym climbing tends to instill a false sense of safety that is dangerous in an outdoor area.

What the beginner should realize is that the best climbers in the world today have been climbing for many years, and most have acquired their experience through traditional methods, by climbing outdoors. Take the time to learn the essential skills that will enable you to climb in any situation safely.

# 2. Modern Climbing Equipment

Less is more.

*— Robert Browning*

Equipment does not make a climber. The first and foremost step in climbing is to equip oneself with technique, footwork, control, and other skills of movement, balance, and strength. These are often developed best in bouldering, then in an apprenticeship with a qualified teacher. Such a teacher will impress upon the student the fact that no amount of equipment is a replacement for ability. Equipment is always only a supplement. Basic equipment includes shoes, rope, chalk bag, a few carabiners, slings, and a harness. After these items, the list becomes attuned to the needs of the climber and the requirements of the rock. A climber selects the equipment needed for the stretch of rock that he or she will climb that day. While there is a certain tendency to carry forty-five pounds of possible protection on every pitch "just in case," most climbers benefit more by carrying the perfect amount of gear and thereby minimizing weight and tangles. Thinking in this sense of safety, it is good to consider that some of what you take away from the sport adds to it. This attitude explains the huge popularity of bolted face climbing.

Over the last ten years there have been many changes in climbing equipment. The introduction and subsequent use of spring-loaded camming devices and micro nuts have inspired many climbers. Today, climbers are succeeding on climbs that were not thought possible just a few years ago. Clean climbing gear continues to improve. Unfortunately, the level of difficulty that is possible using this type of protection has apparently reached a high. This leaves face climbing as the forum for the advancement of climbing difficulty.

The use of permanent anchors has changed the type and amount of equipment needed on many free climbs. A climber need only have a lightweight harness, a pair of shoes, rope, and a half dozen quick draws to climb a route at the highest level of difficulty. This doesn't exclude the use of other types of equipment though. If you are going to a modern climbing area, you may have to use traditional forms of protection in order to set up a climb. It's important for every climber to know how to use all forms of rock protection.

<blockquote>
Knowledge is power.
— Francis Bacon
</blockquote>

## Modern Rock Climbing Shoes

Free climbing requires precise footwork. The type of shoe you wear directly affects your ability to climb well, especially if you don't have strong feet. Feet also need to be protected because of their vulnerability to injury in the event of a fall.

Modern rock shoes are made of a variety of light materials and come in an assortment of styles. Most employ the newest technology in sticky rubber soles. There are three basic types of shoes: the slipper, the high-top, and low-top. They are constructed using two methods, slip last and board last.

### The Sole

Climbing shoes use a sticky rubber that adheres to rock exceptionally well. Every manufacturer uses a different formula in the development of its rubber. One manufacturer, Five Ten, produces rubber specifically for climbing shoes.

### The Rand

The rand surrounding the sole is made of a rubber similar to

**Figure 2-1** Features of a modern rock shoe.

but often not the same as the sole. The best shoe designs have sticky rubber on their rands, for use in cracks and pocket climbing. Some designs have what is called a slingshot rand. This design aids in pushing your foot into the front of the shoe, enhancing the shoe's performance on steep face climbs.

### The Upper

The upper part of a climbing shoe can be made of any number of materials, the most popular being lined leather. Leather will often last much longer than suede or synthetics but is heavier. Shoes with uppers made of unlined leather will stretch and must be fitted especially tight when first bought so that they will not become "sloppy" after a time. If the shoe has a slingshot rand, it will retain its tight fit considerably longer than one with a standard rand.

### Shoe Construction

There are two basic types of shoe construction: *board last* and *slip last*. Board last is the type used in common shoes such as sneakers or street shoes. This type of shoe is made of the following parts: the upper right, the upper left, the tongue, the bottom (with or without some type of insole support), the rand, and the sole.

Slip last shoes, well suited construction for climbing footwear, are designed to fit the foot more like a sock. This type fits exceptionally tight. The upper right and upper left sections connect on the bottom of the shoe, and the rubber sole and rand are glued to the bottom of the upper.

### Shoe Care

The longevity of the shoe depends on how the shoe is cared for. Keep your shoes as clean as possible. The rubber used on climbing shoes is so sticky that any dirt on the sole will compromise the efficiency of the shoe to stick to the rock. Wipe them off on your pantleg or with your hand before you leave the ground, to eliminate the danger of slipping on particles of dirt.

Do not leave climbing shoes in the sun or in any hot place for long periods of time. Shoes use glues that weaken when exposed to extreme heat. Heat will cause them to de-laminate and fall apart. It's a good idea to keep shoes in some type of shoe bag (stuff sack) when not in use.

### Shoes for the Beginner

One of the first purchases a beginner will have to make is a pair of rock climbing shoes. The variety of shoes available nowadays is overwhelming. To get a pair of shoes that will last more than one season, here are a few tips:

Get shoes that have insoles. An insole is a platform made of a rigid or semi-rigid material built into or to be placed in the bottom of the sole. This platform will aid in standing on small holds and help to relieve some of the fatigue associated with standing on toes for long periods of time.

The shoe you choose should have a full rand surrounding the sole. This will give the shoe more versatility while climbing different rock formations. It will also extend the life of the shoe.

The most important thing to consider when choosing a shoe is the fit. Rock climbing shoes are not made to be comfortable for walking, so it is practically impossible to tell if the shoe fits by standing in it. If you have a choice, buy your shoes at a shop that has some sort of climbing wall. This way you can compare

A.

B.

**Figure 2-2**  Rock shoe construction A. Slip last construction. B. Board last
construction.

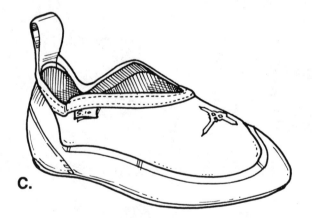

**Figure 2-3**   A. Low top shoe (5.10 Lynx). B. High performance slipper (5.10 UFO. C. Slipper (5.10 Anaszl Moccasin).

several shoes as to how they feel when you climb. You may want to try a different shoe on each foot during this test. Some materials used in the construction of the shoes vary from one manufacturer to the next. Ask the salesperson if and how much the shoe you are interested in will stretch. This will help you to size accordingly. As a general rule, if you intend to climb hard, you will need a tight shoe.

### Shoes for the Intermediate

Someone with a year or two of climbing experience will probably want to get into a more specialized type of shoe or may want to have a couple of pairs for different types of climbing. As I said before, if you intend to climb hard, you will want a tight fit. You don't want the shoe slipping to the sides under your foot. You don't want the toe to be loose. Your toes should be slightly bent into the toe of the shoe. Some shoe types to consider are *slippers, low-top shoes* with or without insoles, and *high-top shoes.* Slippers are good if you train indoors on artificial walls. They aid in strengthening toes and are also great for pocketed face climbing or overhangs on real rock. Low-top shoes are the preferred shoe of most face climbers, although they do not provide protection for the ankles. They are lightweight and well suited to a variety of climbing conditions. Some come with insoles, others do not. High-top shoes are still very popular. The added height protects ankles from abuse, a real plus if you intend to do much crack climbing.

### Shoes for the Expert

The expert climber usually owns several pairs of shoes: a pair of very light slippers for training, a pair of light slippers or a light shoe without an insole for strenuous upper-body face climbing, a pair of light shoes with an insole or insert for hard routes where edging is necessary, and a comfortable pair of medium-weight shoes for long routes. These choices vary from climber to climber. Other expert climbers use one pair of shoes all the time. The trick is finding what works best for you.

> All objects are merely patterns
> in an inseparable cosmic process;
> these patterns are intrinsically dynamic,
> continually changing into one another,
> in a continuous dance of energy.
> — *Fritjof Capra*

**A.**

**B.**

**C.**

**Figure 2-4** Modern climb harness. A. Light weight. B. Medium weight. C. Heavy- duty.

## Harnesses for Climbing

Modern climbing harnesses are constructed of lightweight materials and come in a variety of weights. Lightweight for extreme free climbing, mid-weight for all-around climbing or working on routes, and heavy-duty for big-wall climbing or other heavy work.

The waist belt of the harness may have tie-in loops or be connected by a buckle. Tie-in harnesses are very secure and do not depend on any hardware for their integrity. They are also the lightest. Buckle harnesses are the preferred choice of many climbers because they are easy to adjust. Many trendy styles now come with a buckle connection. The most important thing to consider when choosing a harness is its construction. Many of the largest manufacturers, such as Petzl, have testing facilities which they use in the design of their harnesses.

Lightweight harnesses are adequate for many modern routes. They usually have two to four gear loops on their sides which are ample space for the gear needed on most routes. Extra-light harnesses are available but are primarily for competition climbing and not designed for carrying any amount of equipment. They are, however, nice to have for difficult on-sight climbing and redpoint attempts.

Mid-weight harnesses are good for longer routes or for working routes where you have to spend time sitting in a harness. They often have padded waist belts and leg loops which increase comfort.

Big wall climbing is better with a heavy-duty harness since you often have to hang mass quantities of gear from your harness, especially if you are aid climbing. If you are free climbing on a big wall, you can often get away with a light or mid-weight harness and an over-the-shoulder gear sling or two.

## Chalk and Chalk Bags

While chalk is not necessary for all climbers (some of us don't sweat so much), some cannot do without it. In bouldering, chalk protects the holds from sweat and grease build up and thus contributes to safety as well as rock and route preservation. Chalk bags come in a variety of sizes and shapes. The type you use is personal, but consider the construction and how well it holds the chalk. One method to prevent unsightly chalk spills is the use of a

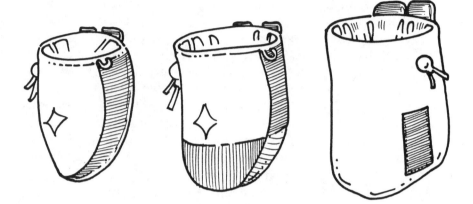

**Figure 2-5**   Chalk bags

bag constructed of light mesh fabric filled with powdered chalk. This keeps the chalk in one place, in your bag.

Many modern face climbers prefer the smaller chalk bags now available. You may want a larger bag if you intend to climb cracks.

## Carabiners and Quick Draws

There are many different types of carabiners on the market today. Some are designed for general climbing, and a few are specifically designed for modern free climbing. Four basic types exist. The classic *oval*, the *D*, the *modified D* and the *locking biner*, which comes on all the aforementioned shapes. All can be used in free climbing, but some are better for specific purposes. Let's start at the bottom of a climb and work our way up, describing the most common uses of carabiners on a modern rock climb.

The carabiner used most often on the harness of a climber is the locking carabiner. This is a link to the belay device used to protect the leader.

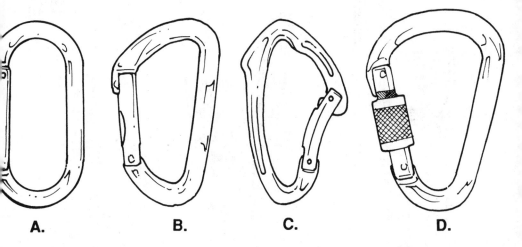

**Figure 2-6** Carabiner. A. Standard oval. B. Modern Light D with key lock gate. C. Modern bent gate D. Large locking carabiner.

The next carabiner used will be one that is placed by the leader on the first piece of protection on the climb.

At the next piece of protection, you may need a quick draw—two carabiners connected by a loop of nylon webbing. The loop may be sewn or tied. A quick draw can be long, or as short as three inches, and allows the rope to run freely in a straight line up the route. This reduces rope drag that would occur if you didn't use one on each piece of protection. A quick draw also reduces the possibility of the rope pulling a piece out of its placement. You can use quick draws (or sling runners) whether you are clipping bolts or using clean protection. There are several quick draw configurations that are beneficial (the last one costs the most and is definitely a specialty item designed primarily for bolt-protected routes):

- an oval carabiner on the top of the quick draw and a "D" shaped carabiner on the bottom
- a modified D/straight gate on the top of the quick draw and a modified D/bent gate on the bottom

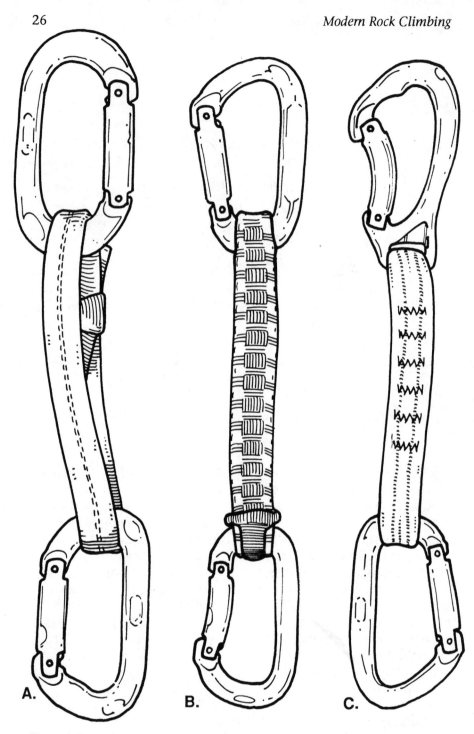

**Figure 2-7**   Quick draw configurations. A. Oval and D.  B. Light D & Light Bent gate D. C. Captive eye.

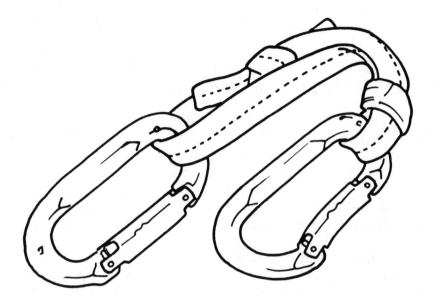

**Figure 2-8**   Supertape Runner.

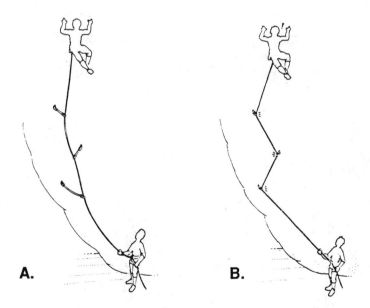

**A.**

**B.**

**Figure 2-9**   A. Runners used to reduce the amount of drage, or friction of the
rope. B. If runners are not used, the amount of drag created in the
system will make it difficult to climb.

- a modified D carabiner on the top and a captive eye carabiner on the bottom

If you are climbing a bolt-protected route, all you need are the correct number of quick draws (one for each bolt) and a couple of long draws for clipping into the anchor at the top of the route.

If you are using clean protection, you are better off using five-foot supertape quick draws doubled with a biner (carabiner) on each end. The extra available length allows you to adjust the draws more easily. Climbs that require clean protection are not as often straight up as most modern bolt-protected routes. Look ahead, and, if the route you are climbing takes a serpentine course, take some long quick draws so you can reduce rope drag.

## Clean Climbing Equipment

By "clean" protection, we mean the type of rock protection that does not harm the rock. Nuts, Hexentrics, SLCDs, and TCUs are all forms of clean protection. Devices such as these are often needed as anchors on climbs. They may have to be used on the ground as belay anchors or on top of a cliff for top rope anchors.

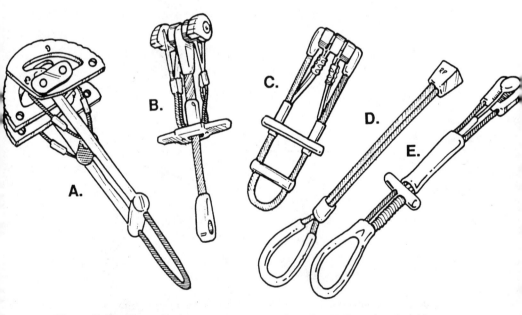

**Figure 2-10**  Clean climbing equipment. A. Camelot. B. Friend with cable system. C. Wired Bliss TCU. D. RP brass nut. E. Lowe/Byrne Ball nut.

Your life depends on the quality of your anchors. Whether you're belaying off two beefy bolts or a few skimpy RPs, you need to know what you're looking at and how it all works. The ability to place protection is not as difficult as the ability to place it correctly. Go out and play on boulders or on a short route that will enable you to place a variety of protection devices. Experiment with a top rope if you don't trust anything you place. Accidents happen because people don't know how to use gear (not because they don't have enough gear). Accidents are also the result of relying on the gadgetry and equipment without having the appropriate climbing skill and technique.

### Nuts

One of the most basic pieces of equipment on a climber's rack is the nut. Nuts come in an assortment of sizes and shapes, from the micro RP to sizes that are several inches wide. The wedge shape nut allows it to be placed in a crack that is slightly tapered.

When you place the nut, it should be set snugly into the crack and given a light tug to set it. Avoid jerking hard on it. This can cause it to become too tightly wedged in the crack, making it difficult to remove. A nut tool is useful, to remove nuts fallen on or too tightly placed. It is common for beginners to overset nuts. Don't feel bad; this has happened to the best of us at one time or another. Oversetting usually signifies a lack of trust in the placement or a high fear factor or simply lack of experience at placing nuts.

### Hexentrics and Other Forms of Protection

Before the development of the spring-loaded camming device, the chock of choice was the Hexentric. Designed by Tom Frost and Yvon Chouinard, a Hex is a nut with a cam-like effect. The offset hexentric shape allows it to be placed in nearly parallel-sided cracks, something that can't be done with a Stopper. Several other types of nuts and variations of the nut are available, but the modern climber will find that they may be troublesome to place on very difficult routes where there is not much time to let go.

Hexentrics are set differently into cracks than other kinds of nuts and at first take a little getting used to because they appear to be setting loosely in the crack. It is helpful if they rest above a constriction in the crack or if the crack is tapered toward its bottom. They do not work well in flaring cracks.

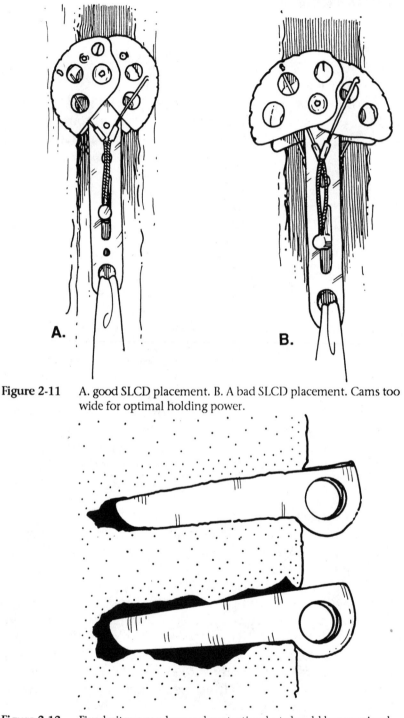

**Figure 2-11**   A. good SLCD placement. B. A bad SLCD placement. Cams too wide for optimal holding power.

**Figure 2-12**   Fixed pitons can be good protection but should be examined closely!

### Spring-Loaded Camming Devices (Friends) (SLCDs)

SLCDs are now among the most useful and popular forms of protection on any climber's rack. They are fast and easy to place, easy and fast to clean. SLCDs started showing up in the early 1980's and have continued to be used with success. There are several brands of SLCDs, the most popular being Wild Country Friends and the Black Diamond Camelot. I suggest some practice before you take any serious runouts on these.

Although one size of SLCD will often fit a wide range of crack sizes, there is an optimum range in which they are designed to be used. To take full advantage of their holding power, understanding correct placement is an important factor. Most manufacturers offer some form of documentation with their product, showing the device's size range and its recommended use.

## Fixed Anchors

Many routes still sport fixed pitons. Although most are safe to clip into, I strongly suggest backing them up if possible. Time and weather and use can cause an old fixed pin to loosen and to become a dangerous and false point of protection. The same goes for old bolts. Never assume that they are bomber! For those of you who don't know this, bolts aren't constructed of some unearthly metal impervious to fatigue. Who the heck places these darn things anyway? Have they placed many bolts? It is possible to screw up a bolt placement and have it look safe. Never trust your life to one point of protection.

All bolts are not created equal. You will soon find that many different types are used on climbs. The best bolts are listed below. Some of the most common you will find are manufactured by Rawl, Hilti, and Petzl.

## Solid-head Sleeve Bolts

The Hilti-HSL bolt is excellent. The HSL comes in zinc-plated steel or solid stainless steel. The bolt does not come with a hanger. This is a very strong bolt suitable for most rock types. Its size is 12x95mm.

Rawl bolts are by far the most commonly used bolt for climbing. They are good for a variety of rock types and are affordable. The Rawl bolt does not come with a hanger, so an appropriate hanger should be selected (considering the placement orientation). Rawl sleeve bolts come in two sizes, 1/2

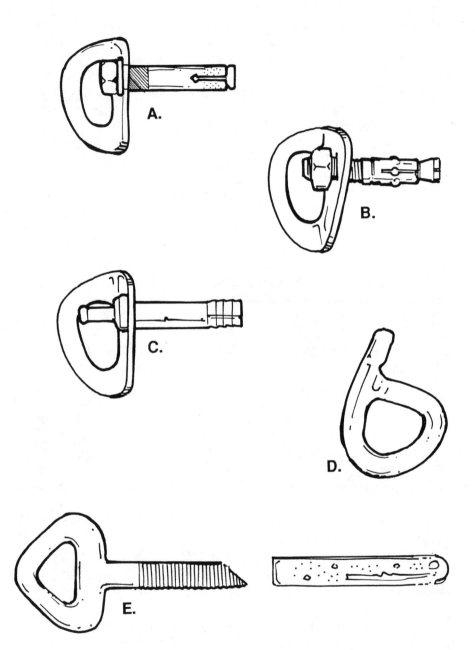

Figure 2-13 A. Rawl solid head sleeve bolt. B. PETZL Coeurgoujon. C. PETZL long life. D. Welded cold shut. E. A glue-in eyebolt.

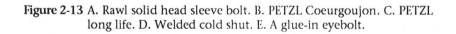

**A.**

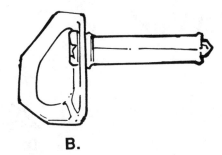

**B.**

**Figure 2-14**    A. Self drive bolt. B. Stardryvn nail bolt

x 3 3/4 inches or 3/8 x 3 inches. They are manufactured in stainless steel or steel with a zinc coating.

Petzl's solid-head sleeve bolt, the Coeurgoujon, is an excellent bolt. It comes with a hanger. The Coeurgoujon is recommended for hard stone only. Its size is 10x61mm.

### Nail Drive Bolts

In hard rock, the Petzl–Long-life is an excellent bolt. It is easily recognizable, because it doesn't have a bolt head. Its size is 1/2 x 2 1/4 inches.

### Other Bolts

Other types of bolts such as wedge bolts, compression bolts, nail drive bolts (Stardryvn), and self-drill bolts should be looked at carefully to assess their integrity. I do not recommend them.

### Bolt Hangers

The hanger is the connecting point between the bolt and your quick draw. A hanger's design dictates its use. Some hangers are designed for less than vertical or vertical rock; others, for rock

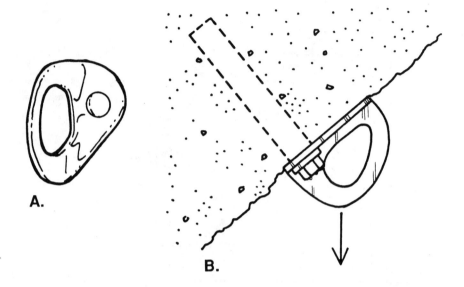

**Figure 2-15** A. A bolt hanger. B. A better way to position the bolt hanger on an overhang.

that is less than vertical to overhanging; and still others primarily for overhanging rock. It is important that the correct hanger be used for each situation.

Bolt hangers should have their strength rating stamped into them. Many, however, do not (hint to all you hanger manufacturers out there), so you will have to do a little research if you're curious.

## Belay Devices

Belaying is one of the most important skills a climber must learn. It is the method of rope management that will connect you and your partner to create a safety system while you climb. Belay anchors are your safety net while climbing. If there are any holes in the system, you could fall through. Many young climbers are becoming spoiled by the proliferation of bolt-protected climbs. Many do not know how to place protection, or if they do are not exactly sure if it's safe.

Learning to place good pro is as important to belaying as is learning to climb. You can learn a few things that will allow you to set a rope on many climbs. When using clean protection for a

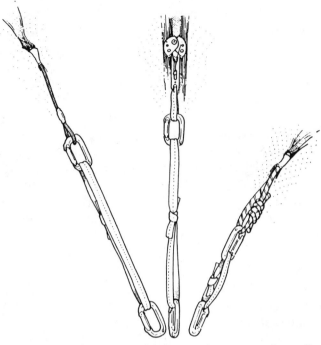

**Figure 2-16** Clean protection used for an anchor. Notice how all pieces are equalized with slings.

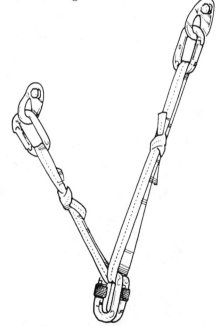

**Figure 2-17** Bolt hangers that are not placed at equal height horizontally should be equalized with slings.

belay anchor, you should place at least three and up to five different pieces of pro and equalize them or place them in opposition so that no one piece will have to take more force than another and so that they hold one another in place.

Belaying in its most primitive form is done in the following way: one end of the rope is tied to you, the other is tied to your partner. The method you use to belay is as simple as wrapping the rope around your waist and feeding it out to your partner as he climbs. If he falls, you hold the rope-thereby stopping your partner from falling. This is the traditional method, not a bad thing to know, and used still by many modern climbers. But other methods are more popular now and mechanically require less strength or burning of clothes.

### *The Sticht Plate*

There are several devices to make belaying easier. A basic belay gadget is the Sticht plate. A Sticht plate-or friction plate as it is sometimes called-allows you to create friction through the device rather than around your waist. Using a belay plate takes a good deal of practice. There are many variations of the Sticht plate, such as the Yates Belay Slave, Lowe Tuber, and the Black Diamond Air Voyager. All employ the same principles and are equally good for belaying.

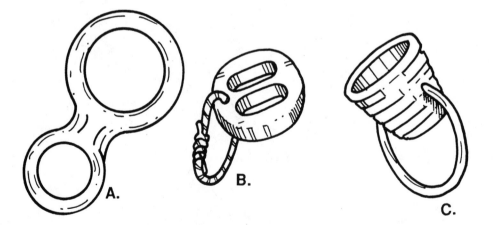

**Figure 2-18**    Belay devices. A. Figure eight. B. Sticht plate. C. Lowe tuber.

### Figure-8 Devices

I see many climbers using figure-8 descending devices for belays. If you must use a figure-8 for belaying, make sure it is one that is made of forged metal. Belaying through a figure-8 descending device also may occasionally cause your rope to twist, a problem that can be reduced by the use of a Sticht plate or similar device made specifically for belaying. Whatever device you choose, know its proper use. Don't assume that because you saw someone else use it the idea is good.

The drawbacks to using a Sticht plate or figure-8 device for belaying on a modern route are: 1) It is difficult to feed rope in and out of the device quickly. This can cause problems on a route that requires quick reactions from the belayer. 2) If the belayer is not experienced enough, rope can slide through the device- increasing the length of a fall or causing rope burns. This problem can be largely eliminated by using one of the new self-actuating belay devices.

### The GriGri

A device called the GriGri made by the French company, Petzl, automatically stops the rope from traveling through it during a fall. It allows beginners with a minimal amount of instruction to be belaying like an expert. Also there are fewer worries for the leader, since the device will automatically lock in the event of a fall.

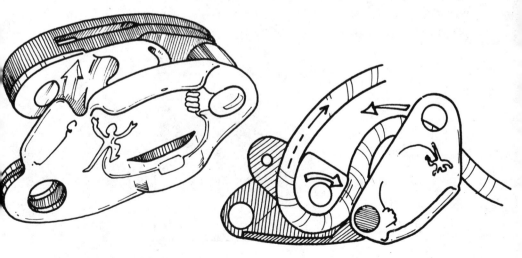

**Figure 2-19**    The PETZL GriGri.

For more advanced climbers, the GriGri enables precise rope control when it is needed. Slack can be fed out and retrieved quickly. The device also works well as a single rope stop descender for route work such as rappell cleaning or bolting. Once you use one of these devices, you might never want to use a belay plate again! You will find the GriGri a worthwhile investment because of its ease of use and the factor of increased safety.

## Ropes

Modern climbing ropes bear little resemblance to ropes used thirty years ago. Besides being stronger, they add a shock absorbing buffer to the protection system.

Climbing ropes come in a variety of lengths and diameters. The length generally used in climbing is 165 feet. You will find this length sufficient for climbing most routes. A few climbers use 180-foot ropes, because the extra length allows them to cut ends off as they wear (without sacrificing the length needed for most routes).

The diameter of a climbing rope is measured in millimeters. The smallest rope that can or should be used for free climbing is an eight or eight and one half-millimeter rope, and the largest is a twelve-millimeter rope. Eight and nine-millimeter ropes are not recommended as single ropes for lead climbing. Ten-millimeter ropes are good general-purpose ropes for leading hard routes and for rehearsals. Large-diameter ropes are especially good for working routes and for top roping, rappelling, cleaning, and preplacing protection, or bolting on rappel.

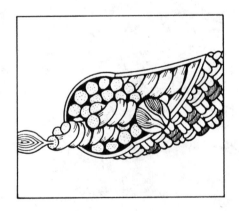

**Figure 2-20**    Kernmantle rope construction

Climbing ropes have a braided synthetic fiber core, surrounded by a braided sheath which protects the core from abrasion. This is called Kernmantle construction. The core is made in such a way that it acts as a shock absorber in the stress of a climbing fall. Such Kernmantle ropes are called *dynamic ropes*. This is the type of rope that should be used for leading and top roping routes.

Another kind of rope is the *static rope*, which does not stretch. Static ropes are good for top roping and rappel bolting or pre-protecting new routes. They make excellent extensions for top roping anchors because they are less susceptible to deteriorating over an edge.

### Rope Care

Your rope is your life line; don't abuse it. The fewer falls it has, the better. When not in use, your rope should be protected from harmful chemicals, heat, dirt, and sharp objects. A rope bag is a good investment. When you're climbing, try to keep your rope out of the dirt. There are a couple of high quality rope bags available that come with a tarp built into them. The tarp is

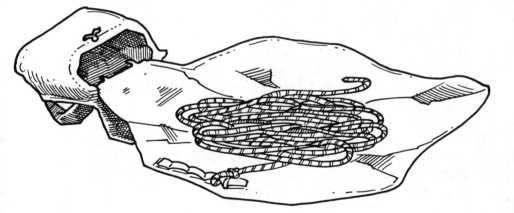

**Figure 2-21**    A modern rope pack/bag.

meant to be wrapped around the rope so that there is no need to coil it. Not only does it keep your rope clean, it gives you a great place to sit and put shoes on.

## Safety Note

Always prevent rope and slings and other equipment from running over sharp edges. Top rope anchors should have extensions if they are running over an edge. A dynamic rope will abrade very quickly over an edge if you fall on it. Don't wait to find out the hard way! Use long pieces of webbing or a double length of static rope for extensions. If there is no way to avoid a rope running over an edge, you might try padding the edge with a pack or small carpet pad.

Always make sure that equipment is placed in such a way that you reduce any odd forces on it. SLCDs with solid stems rarely work in horizontal cracks. Biners should never rest on edges (this will cause them to break).

## Basic Gear List

Many modern routes do not require much in the way of gear, whereas in the old days it was necessary to bring a certain amount of gear to every route in order to climb it. Nowadays you can climb many routes with a pair of shoes, harness, a full-length dynamic rope, and about a dozen quick draws.

It is a good idea, however, to have some selection of clean protection in case you need it. Many climbs do not have permanent anchors at belays. A number of free carabiners, several medium to long runners, a small selection of stoppers, and a set of SLCDs will be more than enough for anchors on most routes. Of course you will need a larger rack if you intend to do longer climbs. Some routes require many of the same size of one particular type of protection.

If you are climbing cracks, and they are parallel and continuous, you may need up to six SLCDs of the same size. Of course not all of us can afford to own that many camming devices. I always ask my pals if I can borrow a few friends.

## The Modern Climber's Bag of Tricks

Climbers have to be prepared for all types of circumstances. There are a number of "tricks" that will help you get off the ground safely.

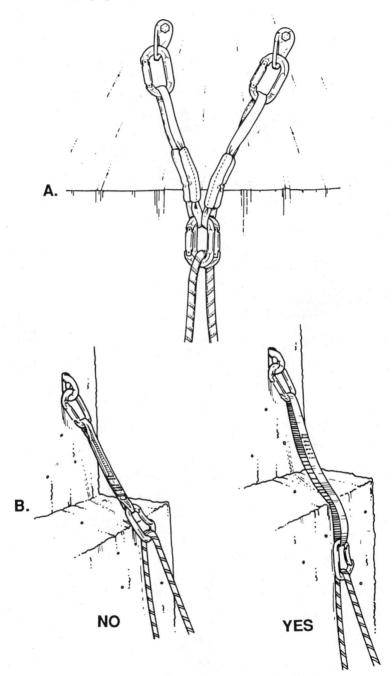

**Figure 2-22**     A. A modern bolt anchor. Webbing tubes are used here to protect the slngs from edge abrasion. B. Always try to prevent carabiners from lying on an edge. Here, this is achieved simply by using a longer runner.

### Cheater Stick

Many modern routes have what appear to be difficult clips right off the ground. If the first bolt of a climb is too high for you to climb to safely, you can use a cheater stick to clip it. A cheater stick is a long tool, hanger wire, whatever to which you attach a quick draw with the rope already clipped into it.

### Biner Saver

If you are climbing a bolt-protected route and are taking repeated falls on the same move, you can avoid damaging a lightweight carabiner by replacing it with a heavy locking biner.

### Improved Prusik

This prusik knot is tied using 9/16 supertape instead of perlon.

### Double Clipping

Double clipping is a way of backing up the single biner that is used to connect a quick draw to a piece of protection. It is a good method of backing up the biner on the first bolt of many modern routes. It (or a locking biner) should be used whenever you face the possibility of a ground fall.

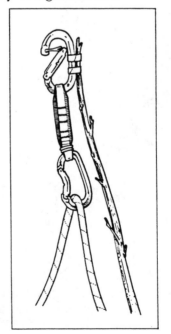

**Figure 2-23**    Stick clip.

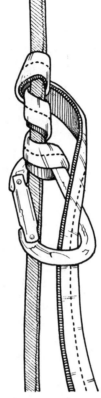

**Figure 2-24**  Improved prusik knot.

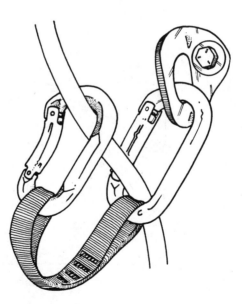

**Figure 2-25**  Double clip.

### *Tying In—Double Bowline versus Figure-8*

The most popular knot used to tie into a climbing harness is the figure-8 knot. A problem with using this knot while working routes is that it can be extremely difficult to untie when it is repeatedly fallen on. A good alternative is to use a double bowline. The double bowline is simple to tie and easily untied after repeated falls, even when your forearms are seriously pumped. Don't forget the backup safety knot!

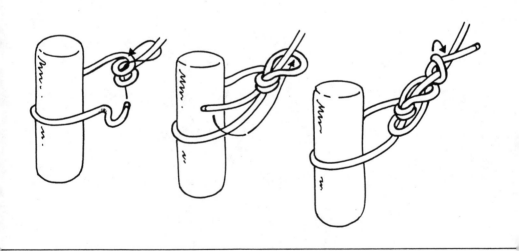

**Figure 2-26**    Double bowline knot.

# 3. GETTING STARTED

We can be knowledgeable
with other men's knowledge,
but we cannot be wise
with other men's wisdom.
               — *Michel de Montaigne*

Getting started in rock climbing is easier now than it has ever been. It is essential to attend at least a few days of a climbing class or to find a mentor with the patience to begin at the beginning. A solid foundation in basic gear placement, rope work and belaying is more important than climbing skill at first. As with any complex sport, excellence is the perfection of fundamentals.

## Warming up before Climbing

Have you ever heard a friend say he can't go climbing because of muscle fatigue, sore fingers, or some other painful injury? Ailments such as these are common among climbers, especially those who don't stretch regularly or don't warm up before climbing.

Many climbers do not realize the importance of a good warm-up. In their excitement, they often go to the crags and hop onto the hardest route of the day. This can lead to serious injury. Try holding your hands in front of you and extend and retract your fingers about fifteen times. Then shake them out for about the same period of time. Repeat this until your hands are warmed up. Stretch foot, calf, and other leg muscles. Start out on climbs that allow you to work up to your maximum potential. Use easier climbs as warm-ups, taking small breaks between each, until you are warmed up and ready to work on the hardest route you wish to climb for the day. Avoid warming up on routes that require the use of pebbles or small finger holds, if you can.

When you are climbing in a gym, an excellent way to warm up is to walk around the base of the climbing wall and grab each hold. Move along the wall, pulling slightly on each hold. Don't hang from the holds until you feel your fingers beginning to warm up. As they warm up, do short vertical problems using large holds. It is vitally important at this point to listen to your body. Warming up takes time, and if you jump the gun you will regret it later. The harder you intend to climb, the longer and more intense your warm-up should be. At the Skinner gym, a good warm-up can take from one to two hours.

**Figure 3-1**  Warming up to climb. Move from hold to hold without doing pull ups or hangs.

**Figure 3-2**  Always have a friend spot you if you are less than an expert and are
bouldering.

## Bouldering

Climbing boulders is a wonderful way to become familiar with climbing. A single boulder can offer a variety of routes covering a wide range of difficulty. It is possible to spend days or even years working on the endless number of problems that exist in a single boulder field. Bouldering builds confidence in your ability to execute extremely technical moves. You can practice very difficult moves with a relative amount of safety-moves that you might not try on a lead route.

When bouldering, have someone spot you if there is any chance of a fall. Many serious injuries in climbing have occurred by jumping or falling from boulder problems.

## Basic Top Roping

Top roping is a safe method of bouldering or roped climbing, requiring little equipment. By running a rope through an anchor at the top of a climb, you can safely set up a top belay. This is advisable on boulders as well as short routes that need the added safety of a rope. Top roping is a common method of rehearsing very difficult routes, and there are several systems that are of importance to the modern climber. A basic single rope top rope can be set up on many climbs with a minimum amount of trouble.

## Advanced Top Rope Techniques

Most top ropes are relatively simple to set up. Occasionally you may have to use more than one rope (or even three or four). There are also several setups that are beneficial for working on overhanging routes.

### Long routes that require two ropes

You may wish to use two ropes tied together when working a long route, but it is not advisable. A modern dynamic rope stretches so much that, in the event of a fall, a climber could hit the ground while climbing the lower section of a route. This stretch factor is increased when two ropes are tied together. The alternative is to use two full-length static ropes.

If the route is overhanging, the rope should be run up and through the anchors and then back down the route clipped through the quick draws or other protection on the route. The climber should tie into the rope that runs through the quick

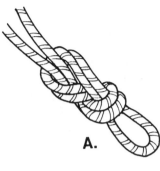

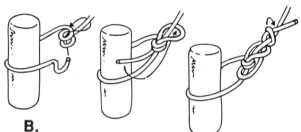

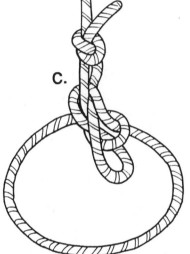

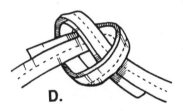

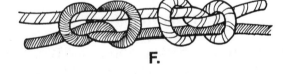

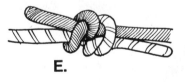

**Figure 3-3** Important climbing knots. A. Figure eight knot. B. Double bowline, C. Single bowline with backup knot. D. ring bend. E. Double overhand. F. Double fisherman's knot.

draws. This will keep him/her close to the wall in the event of a fall.

On shorter routes (those under seventy-five feet), the system is much simpler but almost the same as the aforementioned. Care must be taken here that the climber does not hit the ground due to rope stretch. It is the belayer's duty to be very attentive in this situation.

Climbing the route and then hanging or taking a practice fall will take some of the stretch out of the system.

A top rope system can also be set up after a climber has led a route. After lowering, the lead rope can remain clipped through all the quick draws, and then the second can tie into the rope that runs up and through the quick draws.

## Knots

Tying into a climbing rope and securing yourself to the rock require the use of several knots. The following paragraphs describe the most commonly used knots and how to tie them. It is important that knots untied often, or those that are fallen on repeatedly, can be undone easily.

### Figure-8 knot

This knot can be used for many purposes while climbing. It is currently the most common knot taught to beginners, as the knot to tie into the climbing harness. The figure-8 knot can be tied anywhere in the length of a rope but can be difficult to untie if a fall is taken on it.

### Double Bowline Knot

This knot is used as a tie-in by many climbers. It must be tied with a backup knot. This is a good knot to use if the rope is going to be taking a lot of weight from falling or rope work. It unties easily. Do not clip into the loop of a bowline.

### Bowline on a Bight

This is a bowline that can be tied in the middle of the rope or anywhere along the length of a rope. It is handy for third parties on a single rope or for a big tie-in loop at multiple anchor belays.

### Modified Single Bowline Knot

This is easy to tie, is light, and it unties easily. It works well as a tie-in knot.

WARNING! Always tie a backup knot when using a bowline.

### Ring Bend (Overhand Thread)
This is the knot most commonly used to connect two pieces of webbing together in the making of a sling or in tying two ropes together for a rappel.

### Clove hitch
The clove hitch is a simple knot that allows adjustments in the belay tie-in, making it very useful at belays or in multiple-anchor situations. A clove hitch can be tied anywhere in the length of a rope.

### Grapevine knot
The grapevine is used to tie two pieces of rope together, also used to connect the ends of perlon on slung nuts. It can be used to tie two ropes together for rappelling, or for double rope top ropes, but can be difficult to untie if it is fallen on.

### Overhand
This is a quick and easy knot to use to tie in at an anchor. An overhand can be tied in the middle or along the length of a rope but is hard to break once it is set by a fall or body weight.

Always tie directly into your climbing harness. Do not use a carabiner (any type!) between you and the climbing rope.

## Moving on the Rock
All of the techniques of climbing should be learned and built upon, much as a dancer builds a repertoire of dance moves. Each type of move or technique can be customized to your personal style of climbing. Learning how to climb a modern route is often like learning the choreography of a dance.

### Balance
Balance is an important aspect of free climbing. Find your center and focus on it while you climb. If you can center, your body will tell you which way to turn or where you should place your weight to gain the optimum position for ease of progress.

### Static Moves
A static move is one that is performed with at least three points in contact with the rock.

### Dynamic Moves

A dynamic move is basically an all-out lunge for a hold where the body loses most (or all) of its contact with the rock.

### Dead Point

A dead point is a controlled dynamic move. The hold that you are dead pointing to is the target. A controlled lunge is made for the target, and at the highest point of the lunge it is grabbed or hit. Since a dead point is more controlled than a dyno, the target can be very small.

### Footholds

Good footwork is the true foundation of good technique. It also allows you to save much of your power for sections of the climb where you will need it the most.

#### Smearing

Smearing is used most often on friction climbs, or climbs with no footholds or edges, but is often a technique also applied to small holds on steep rock and overhangs. The rubber on modern rock shoes is specifically designed for this use. The part of the shoe used for smearing is the front of the sole under the toes. You don't necessarily need an edge. You can smear on almost any rock feature. The smallest bulge on a face can become an excellent foothold if used correctly.

Friction climbing requires that the climber use his body weight to hold the bottom surface of his shoes on a holdless, smooth section of rock. It is important to keep your weight over your feet and move smoothly up the rock. You should look for hand holds. But if they are not readily available, use an open hand on the rock to keep your body out and away from the rock. Weight over feet! A palm-down hand position can be useful if you need to push yourself up a steep section.

#### Edging

Often the rock is too smooth or steep to smear effectively. You must look for edges to stand on. Climbing, using the smallest edges, requires precision footwork. Toes must be placed carefully and confidently. Once placed, the foot should remain in the effective position throughout the move. You will also find the outside edge of the shoe to be useful.

*Pockets*

Since pockets are formed at or beneath the surface of the rock, it is often difficult to see them once you move above. You must look for the pockets as you climb past them and remember where they are.

*Hooking*

It is often possible to stabilize yourself during a difficult move by hooking your toe on, behind, or under a feature of rock.

*Heel Hooking*

Heel hooking is a very helpful technique when climbing overhangs. By placing your heel over your head and hooking it on an object, you can take a great deal of stress off the arms and can aid in pulling higher.

### *Handholds*

When you were a child, you may have loved to climb trees. When you climbed trees, you followed the path of least resistance from the largest branch to the next. You used the largest branches, because they are the strongest. Climbing rock is similar. At the basic level you climb using the largest holds you can reach, paying little attention to the style you use getting from one to the next, and quite often forgetting to use your feet to help push you up.

As your climbing skills improve, you learn to pay closer attention to the details of how to use holds and footholds because they are not always as big as you like. You will find that as you get stronger and climb harder the small holds become just as important and useful as the big holds.

On large holds, the technique is fairly self-explanatory. Grab the hold and pull. When using small holds, you must refine your technique. Hand and finger position are important.

Small holds, or "crimpers," can be used by placing the flat pads of the fingertips on the hold or the tips (ends) of the fingers (straight down). Keep your fingers pulled into your palm. Your thumb can be used to strengthen this grip by placing it over your index finger.

The open-hand grip is just what it sounds like. Your fingers lay on the hold, your palm open on the rock. This is effective for sloping holds and small pocket climbing.

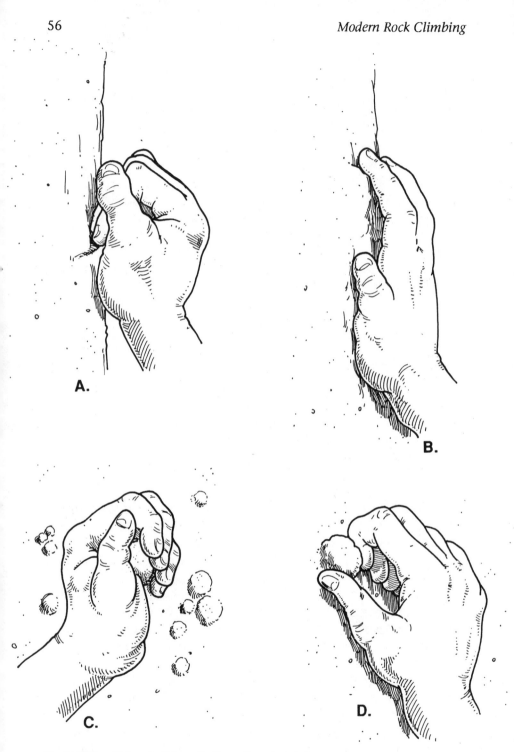

**Figure 3-4**     Grips. A. Crimp. B. Opendhand. C. Wrap. D. Pinch.

*Stemming*

The basic stemming position, standing with your feet in opposition between two rock faces, occurs often in climbing-often serving as a means of rest. A stem can, however, be executed in positions other than in a corner. The X position is one of the most effective positions for difficult climbing, being stable and allowing you to rest.

*Side Pulls*

Side pulls seem a bit foreign at first but greatly add to one's repertoire of climbing moves. When using large holds or a crack to pull on, this technique is called a lieback. You use your arms to pull and your feet in opposition to push, as you move them up the rock. Liebacks and side pulls require precise balance. Any vertical hold can be used as a side pull. The side pull can be used while climbing pocketed faces, edge climbs, aretes, cracks, just about anything.

*Underclings*

Holds that face (or hang) down are called underclings. Large underclings are a welcome break on a route that is primarily made up of pull downs. They allow you to use a different muscle group and occasionally offer an opportunity to rest. Small underclings are more difficult but can often be found.

*Pinch*

The pinch grip is important on a lot of routes. It is a good grip to work on in the gym and will add to the overall strength of your hand and fingers. A pinch can be narrow or wide.

*Cracks*

Crack climbing involves some strength but more technique. It requires skill and experience to become a good crack climber. Power is required for cracks that are more than vertical, but unfortunately there are not a lot of methods other than climbing cracks that will allow you to gain the experience or the power. Improving your crack climbing technique will take patience, determination, and practice on top-rope routes. Some of the most beautiful routes in the world follow cracks. It is well worth the time to learn on and experience these climbs.

The method used to climb cracks is called jamming. A hand jam is a jam using the hand like a blade. The hand is placed into the crack and expanded. Jamming takes a good bit of practice until you learn how much force is necessary to make the jam work. Different rock types require different techniques as well. A fist jam is performed by clenching the fist horizontally in a crack. As you have probably noticed there are jamming techniques for various sizes of cracks. The smallest jams require tedious finger jamming. The largest are climbed using almost all parts of the body together, i.e. an arm bar, a side-pull, a knee jam, heel-and-toe jam.

A thumbs-up hand position while using the hand, fist or finger jams will give you a different type of leverage. It will take some practice to learn what is best in a given situation—it is all technique.

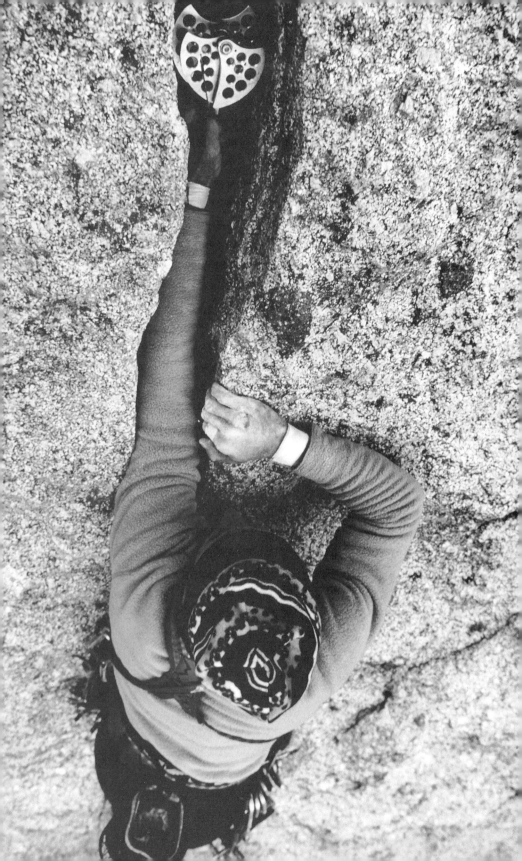

# 4. Modern Climbing Techniques

Grace is the absence
of everything that indicates
pain or difficulty,
hesitation or incongruity.

— *William Hazlitt*

Whether you are a born climber or complete bumbly, mileage on the rock is your best friend. Every move you make on a boulder, face, or wall will add to your skill level and be of help sometime in the future. No matter how great your face climbing ability is, you will not be a good crack climber until you have climbed many cracks. Concentrating only on desperate bolted routes will not add to your expertise in gear placement. If you have mastered the basic skills, you can learn more from experience than anyone can teach you. Mileage, mileage, mileage!

## Ascent Style

Free climbing style is separated into three main levels of purity. In order of highest quality they are the on-sight, the flash, or the redpoint. Several of these ascent styles require practicing the route before it can be climbed, but the end result of each is that the climb was done without falling.

**Figure 4-1**    Free climbs which require the use of clean protection also demand
planning and the skill or knowledge needed to place protection
confidently.

Often, to achieve success on a modern route, you will have to work on the moves. You can do this in several different ways. You can top rope the route-rehearsing the moves before you attempt to lead it. This may help you get enough confidence to lead the route from the ground.

You can preclip quick draws to protection and practice the climbing from the ground, working on the moves between each bolt. When you reach a bolt, you can clip in and rest if you need to. Routes that are overhanging sometimes require a bit more ingenuity.

You can attempt the redpoint and if not successful go back to the first method.

The bottom line is, if you can't achieve a no-fall ascent, you haven't succeeded in actually free climbing the route.

## Definitions of Ascent Styles

### On-sight (Lead)
One of the purest styles that can be achieved when attempting a route is an on-sight ascent. An on-sight is a no-fall lead ascent without prior knowledge of the moves involved on the route. Achieving an on-sight of an extremely hard route nowadays is very difficult, due to the technical sequences involved. However, an on- sight ascent of any route remains the ideal of a climber.

### Flash (Lead)
A flash ascent is close to an on-sight in style. It includes prior knowledge of the route but no rehearsal.

### Flash (Top Rope)
The climber can have prior knowledge of the route but no rehearsal. Even though it is not lead climbing, a top rope flash is still considered a high achievement.

### Redpoint (Lead)
A redpoint is a no-fall ascent, with prior knowledge of the moves involved on the climb. This includes rehearsals and getting *beta* from other climbers. Beta is a technical description of the moves involved on a climb. With good beta, a climber can visualize the sequences on the route before attempting it and often will succeed in redpointing it with very few tries.

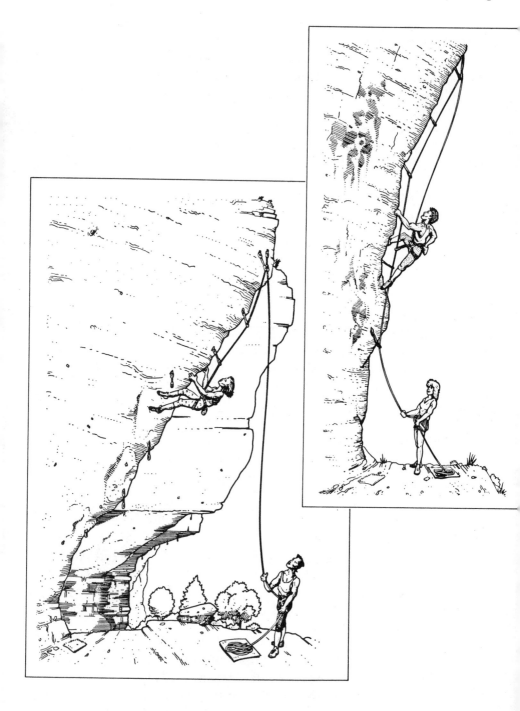

**Figure 4-2**  Advanced top rope techniques.

### *Free Solo (Free Climbing without a Rope)*

The only style that could possibly top an on-sight ascent of a route at your limit is a free solo. Free soloing involves climbing a route without a rope for safety. Soloing a route at the limits of ability is an exciting event. However, soloing is exceptionally dangerous and is not recommended.

## Reaching Your Goals

One of the greatest aspects of climbing is freedom. Your goals as a climber are often what dictate the style of climbing that you pursue. Many climbers choose to climb traditionally, some combine tradition with modern, and some choose modern climbing only. A few don't have any idea what they're doing but know they're having a darn good time doing it-whatever it is.

If you want to try routes that are too difficult for you to lead, or you need to learn some techniques that will allow you to work a route, the following techniques might be helpful. These are methods used by all climbers no matter what their level of difficulty.

## Top Roping

This is probably the safest way to work on a route. A basic top rope setup is easy to arrange on most short climbs. An anchor must be set at the top of the route, as close to the finish as possible. Many modern routes have anchors permanently placed at the end of each pitch. (If you have to set your own anchors, you may want to read the anchor setup section of chapter 2.) Position the rope so that it doesn't run over any sharp edges. Always reverse the gates of the attaching carabiners, or use locking biners if you have them. The climbing rope runs from the ground up, through the anchor carabiners, and back to the ground. One end of the rope is tied directly into the climber's harness, and the other runs through a belay device on the belayer's harness.

### *Top Roping Safety Tips*

- Use a locking carabiner with a heavy standard carabiner where the top rope attaches to the anchor. Many climbers use two or three nonlocking types with the gates reversed. This is fine if you do not have a locking biner.

- Never rely on a single anchor or a single sling or a single carabiner. Eliminate any place in the anchor set-up where everything depends upon only one of these.
- Keep the rope, slings, and carabiners from lying on or running over sharp edges. If anything is running over an edge, rearrange it so it is not (or pad the edge).
- Be aware of objects on the ground or the ground itself that you may hit in the event of a fall. If you are top roping on an overhang, you may swing out and away from the rock. A fall in this situation can be fast and hard. If you are not prepared, you can hit something (such as a tree) and get injured seriously.

## Previewing, Preclipping, and Working a Route

If you have already attempted to on-sight a route with no success and wish then to give it a redpoint attempt, you may want to get some more information about it. Ask others about the moves involved on the climb, or you may want to rappel down the route to look at the moves.

Climbers who are trying a difficult route will often take a peek at the holds prior to attempting a route. By previewing, a climber can get some idea of the movement involved and formulate a plan for his ascent.

Very often during this preview, quick draws are attached to the bolt hangers. This saves time and energy needed for working the route. Any time spent previewing, preclipping, or attempting the route is considered "working a route." Many of the hardest climbs in the world are worked until a redpoint ascent can be made.

When top roping a route that is overhanging, clip one end of the rope through the quick draws that you will have to clip during the lead. This will keep you from swinging out and away from the rock if you fall.

If, after top roping the route you find that there is a particular move you need to work on, focus on it. Use whatever means necessary to get to this section and practice the move until you get it. Be sure you practice the complete route, including the places you will rest.

Routes that have horizontal overhangs can be difficult to work on. When you fall, you may end up too far out from the rock to regain holds. If this happens you can "spring," or "boing," your way back up to your last piece of clipped protection. To execute this maneuver, the leader grabs the rope above, pulling down, creating a loop of loose rope. The belayer, in the meantime, is pulling, or putting full body weight on the rope to the leader. When the leader lets go of the rope, it springs taught leaving the leader higher and the belayer hopefully not on the ground. Repeat as many times as necessary to regain the roof holds.

Working routes is a fairly common practice for the modern climber. It is important to balance the number of routes that you work on with a good number of on-sights and redpoints so you will improve your overall climbing abilities.

## Belaying

Belaying is the method climbers use to safeguard one another with the rope, feeding out or taking in rope and holding the rope in the event of a fall. While one person is climbing, the other is belaying. This is an important job, and the belayer should be very attentive as to what the climber is doing at all times. The relationship between a belayer and the leader can mean the difference between success or failure. It can also be the difference between leaving the rock healthy or injured.

### *Belay Devices*

As discussed in chapter 2, there are several mechanical devices that make belaying easier. There are numerous copies of the original Sticht plate, all are about the same. The Lowe Tuber and Black Diamond Air-traffic Controller are two belay devices that work well. Another option, made by Petzl, is the GriGri, an automatically locking belay device that after a little getting used to makes belaying very simple. It is by far the best and safest belay device made, as of this writing. Petzl is always coming up with innovative ideas for climbing equipment, and it's worthwhile to keep an eye on what they are working on for the future.

### *Belay Positions*

The belayer should always assume a solid, braced position. Always be prepared to catch a fall, and you will not be caught off guard. Stand or sit close to the first piece of protection used by the leader. This is especially important on the lower part of a

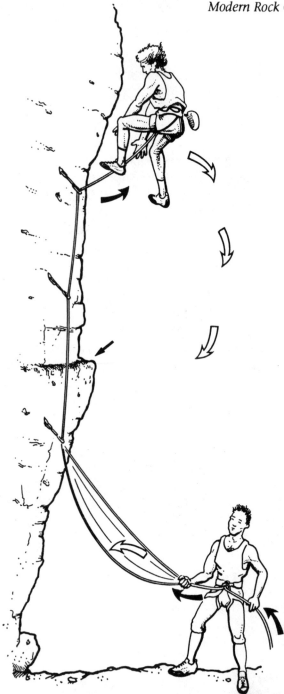

**Figure 4-3**   Your belayer can assist you in avoiding injury if aware of the obstacle you need to avoid. Here the belayer is paying out slack so the climber will not hit a ledge.

route where the rope stretch may allow the leader to hit the ground or where the angle of the rope may affect the placement of the protection. Always listen closely to what the leader is saying and don't debate.

If you are lighter than the person you are belaying, it is a good idea to set up an anchor that will keep you from being pulled off your stance. In fact, a belay should almost always be anchored in such a way-unless standing on the ground and where there is plenty of friction through the protection or through the top belay anchors. Minimize the slack in the rope, to minimize the length of the climber's fall. Almost always provide a static belay-holding the rope tight in a fall and not letting out slack. Today's ropes will stretch the small bit necessary to absorb the fall. Only pay out slack when the force generated by a lead fall might cause the protection to fail, or if letting the falling leader fall past a protrusion of rock. The more energy that is absorbed in the system, the less force will be generated on the protection anchors; and the more protection, the less force on the rope and belayer.

Look at the direction of the rope between you and the first piece of protection. This is the direction you will be pulled up in the event of a fall. If you plan ahead, this pull will probably be no problem. If you are standing facing another direction, you will be jerked around and caught off guard. This could cause injury to you and serious injury to the leader. Basically, pay attention to what you're doing.

If you are climbing very long pitches or multipitch routes, the belay end of the rope should be tied to the belayer's harness after it is run through the belay device. This is to prevent the rope from pulling through the belay device if there is a serious fall or the device fails. Belays should be set up in such a way that the transition from one climber leading to the next leader is smooth and safe.

## Leading a Route

There are several important skills that should be mastered before setting out to lead a climb. Gain experience climbing with another climber who has more experience than you. Watch him carefully and learn from his actions.

- Learn to place and clip protection confidently and securely.

- Learn to take controlled falls. That is, know where you're going to land, consider the direction you will go, and place protection accordingly. Always take into account rope stretch, and avoid long or head-first falls.
- Practice top roping routes that are within and beyond your abilities to estimate your present skill level.
- Learn to belay from above. As a leader, you will be responsible for belaying your partner up as he follows you. Belay setup involves placing secure protection, for the second person (such as on traverses), correctly anchoring yourself, and learning rope management.

Once you have mastered these skills, you will be ready to lead. Yet a number of very easy leads will be necessary as you work up to this level of mastery.

### Some Things to Arrange before Leaving the Ground

Plan ahead! Tie in safely and check your harness and rope. Take enough gear. Set it up on your rack or harness so that it will be easy to get to, and in an  order that you understand. Don't forget what you will need for a belay at the end of the pitch. Check your belay and belayer before starting. Take your time and THINK.

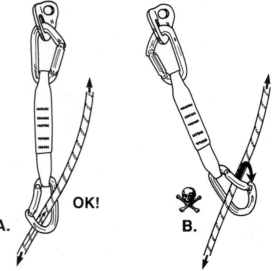

**OK!**

**A.**

**B.**

Figure 4-4    A. Correct. The rope should be clipped into the quick draw exactly as shown. B. Incorrect! If the rope is clipped into a quick draw like this, it is possible for the rope to fall over the gate, opening it and releasing the rope.

## Placing Protection versus Clip-up Routes

Routes that require the placement of gear are quite different than those that require only clipping quick draws. A plan must be made as to what gear you will need for a particular route. Look as far up the route as you can and then take a variety of gear to cover the sections you can and cannot see. On longer routes, if there is any doubt as to what you will need on pitches ahead, put some extra gear in a pack to be carried by your partner. There is a fine line between too much and not enough. You will get a sense for this through experience.

Routes that require the placement of gear are generally more adventurous than those that do not. A basic climbing rack should include:

- One set of small nuts such as RPs
- A full set of wired or slung stoppers or other wedge-type nuts
- One set of SLCDs from .5 through 3 inches
- Ten to fifteen quick draws
- Several runners of varied lengths-up to shoulder-loop length
- Two locking carabiners
- Four to six free carabiners

Having this selection at all times will enable you to do or set up most climbs. If you intend to climb cracks that require more of one size of a particular piece of gear, you should plan accordingly. Climbing partners are always a good source for gear that you may need for a specific climb.

## How to Rest

Learning how to rest while you climb is essential. Not many climbers can power through a route at the limit of their ability without getting a rest. Even routes that do not appear to have rests must be "moved through" in such a way that you do not use all your energy before you get to the top. Small rests can be found if you know how to take them. The "thumbs" rest is an effective rest allowing you to relax your fingers. Underclings or various types of grips use different muscles. If you use a variety of grips you will not burn out as fast.

Hang from your arms without pulling. And on steep rock, keep arms straight whenever possible. You can conserve strength for more difficult climbing. Whenever you hang for a moment from a good hold, don't pull on it, just hang. Take a

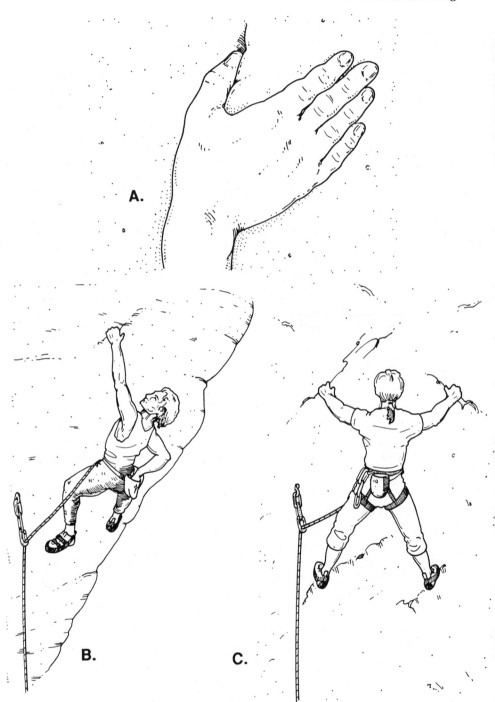

**Figure 4-5**   A. Thumbs rest, hand position. B. Straight arm rest, body position. C. The X body position.

second to relax and concentrate on the move ahead. Look up and find another hold that you can rest from. Move to that hold and rest. Stems are good positions for resting. You can often get a no-hands rest in a good stemming position. Maintain a balanced X position whenever you can. Keep moving if there are no "full body" rests.

### Moving Efficiently on the Rock

Your movement while climbing, if done efficiently, will enable you to rest more effectively. Proper balance with fluid and controlled movements takes much less energy. A common problem for many climbers is that the fear involved in climbing causes them to overgrip holds, and so they get "pumped." Try to use holds only for balance. Pull on them only if you have to pull on them. Of course if the climb is very difficult you will have to be in better shape, because you will have to pull on more holds.

### When to Rest

Get a rest whenever you can. Never pass a rest position unless you know that stopping will cause you more harm than good or destroy your rhythm. Plan your rests as you move up the climb. Look ahead and decide where you will rest before you move. Make your rests brief. If you hang out on an arm rest too long, you will only become more pumped and increase your chance of failure.

> Courage is the resistance to fear,
> mastery of fear, not absence of fear.
> — *Mark Twain*

## Falling

Some climbers never fall. They are always climbing within their limits, and that's okay if that is your personal aesthetic and if you are happy with the level of difficulty at which you are climbing. If, however, you desire to improve your climbing ability, you should attempt to climb some routes that are at least a little harder than those that you can lead confidently. If you do this, you will eventually fall. Falling is definitely scary the first time. Especially if you take a good long one, or "whipper," as they are often called. There are a few things you can do that will take some of the fear out of falling.

**Figure 4-6    Falling**

- Always climb on a rope that is in good condition. This means climb on your own rope or one that you know has been taken care of. Do not climb on a rope that is questionable.
- You need to trust your belayer. Get familiar with your partner's belay experience and let him know what you expect from him-before you leave the ground.
- Learn as much as you can about all types of anchors. This includes clean climbing protection, pitons (you may run into one that is fixed, and you'll feel better about clipping it if you know what it is), bolts and bolt hangers. The more you know about an anchor, the better you'll feel about the possibility of falling on it.
- Be aware of protrusions of rock you may hit if you fall. Look for ledges that you might land on or graze in the event of a fall. If your belayer is aware of these potential collision points, he can plan slack or tension accordingly. Know where you are going to fall. If you are traversing on a pitch and are above your last piece of protection, you will pendulum when you fall. If you are prepared for this, it may not be so bad.
- Be extremely careful about grabbing the rope. In fact, don't touch it unless you have to. If you grab the rope that is coming up from the belayer you can burn your hands badly.
- Keep your hands and feet in front of you for some protection, but don't lock them or you might break something. Try to sit into your harness as you fall. Let the harness, knot, and rope absorb the shock of the fall.

### Practice

Taking little controlled falls will give you a better idea of what to expect. Do this under absolutely safe conditions, such as from a top rope or if leading from several really bomber pieces of protection. Taking a little well-protected fall before you get too high on a route will relieve much of the tension associated with falling and the fear of the unknown.

### After Falling

A climbing rope can absorb the shock of a fall very effectively.

The knot that is tied into your harness also acts as another shock-absorbing link between you and your belayer. You should untie this knot and retie it often if you are falling on it. This is an often overlooked factor in modern climbing and should be given more attention.

> Life consists of what a man
> is thinking all day
> — *Ralph Waldo Emerson*

## Visualization, Beta, and Memorizing Moves

Visualization is a very important tool in climbing. When used, visualization will aid you in accomplishing climbs that you do not yet believe you can do. The first step in this process is to believe, and see yourself succeeding.

### How It Works

Visualization is a method of seeing yourself doing something before you have actually done it. It can be a way of believing in yourself, your power, your strength, and creating an image in your mind that will help you perfect your moves and your balance. Visualization can aid in many aspects in any sport. You must believe you can accomplish your goals before you will accomplish them. The harder the goal, the more important visualization will be.

There are many different techniques or points that you can focus on when visualizing. If you are going to use visualization as an aid for a specific climb, you should first practice the moves of the climb-memorizing them to create a map in your mind. Be sure to include the rests and clips involved. While you are at the cliff, or later at home, you should visualize yourself climbing the route smoothly with power and control. Dream the route and live it.

For on-sight climbing, it may help to visualize yourself as being stronger, lighter, and more powerful.

It is best to practice your visualizing technique in a quiet place where you can concentrate on the objective completely. Some climbers are so focused, however, that they can do it right at the cliff and succeed.

## Advanced Moves for Climbing

The harder you climb, the more your understanding of technique will be required of you. You will find that to move smoothly through all levels of rock terrain, you must build a large repertoire of moves that can be recalled at any given moment. Building this stock of moves can only be done by accumulating mileage on the rock, by climbing longer routes, or bouldering, and in the climbing gym.

### Back Stepping

Back stepping is an important technique in climbing. A back step is the use of the outside edge of the foot on holds below or behind you. Back stepping allows you to use holds that are not reasonable to use with the inside of your foot and by so doing maintain a comfortable balanced position.

### Figure-4

This is a pretty handy technique for use on overhanging rock. It involves putting your leg over your arm at the wrists or at the elbow. Use your leg to push you up so that you can get the next hold with your other hand. This is a nice option when you can't dyno.

**Figure 4-7**    The figure four. This move allows you to make long static reaches that would be difficult to make otherwise.

### Flagging

Flagging is a technique used to improve balance on barn door moves or side cling moves that are difficult. It basically entails using the foot that is not active on a hold, putting it behind you and touching or pushing off of the wall for balance.

### Diagonalling

This is a body position where one hand and the opposite foot are in line. This move can be executed with the inside or the outside of your foot. This type of body position allows for a better reach to holds located diagonally above. Using the outside of your foot in the "knee drop" position is extremely effective on steep overhangs. The hip rotation involved in this move is an important technique.

### Pocket Technique

When using pockets, you can improve two-finger holding power by keeping your index and pinkie fingers down with your thumb. The same goes for mono-doight moves. Hold the fingers that are not being used with your thumb.

Pocket climbing requires very strong fingers. Dedication to fingerboard workouts will greatly improve your pocket climbing ability. Before climbing on pockets, tape and warm up your fingers.

## The End of the Pitch

It is important to be especially careful when you intend to lower from anchors. Since sometimes the rope must be untied from your harness and threaded through an anchor, you are putting yourself in a vulnerable position if you do not do several things in order.

- Communicate exactly what you are doing to your belayer. Repeat yourself until you are absolutely sure that he understands what you are doing and when you are going to do it. If it helps, discuss your signals to him before you start. This is especially important if climbing with a partner with whom you are unfamiliar.
- Be sure that you are clipped into two different anchors and that those are attached directly to your harness, before you untie. Never clip into a single bolt if you can avoid it.

**Figure 4-8**　　Diagonalling. By centering your weight over one foot and using the other as a counter balance, you can achieve long diagonal reaches. Here a side pull is used to increase the reach.

- Before you untie from your harness, pull up some slack and tie off a section of rope so you don't drop it while you are untying and threading the rope through the anchors. Thread the rope through the anchor points and retie to your harness. Pay extremely close attention to your knot as you retie it.
- Always thread the rope through two or three anchors before lowering, especially if you plan to top rope the route. Never thread the rope through sling material alone, as the rope will burn and cut through it.

If the anchor point is large enough, thread a bight of rope through the anchor before you untie from your harness. Tie a figure-8 in the bight after you have passed it through and clip this directly into your harness with a large locking carabiner. Then you can untie the other knot.

Many accidents seem to occur while climbers are preparing to lower from routes or while they are lowering. Some of these could have been avoided if the climbers had paid closer attention to details and not been in a hurry.

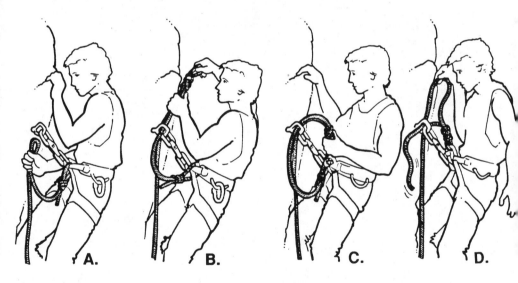

Figure 4-9    Threading the anchor at the end of a pitch. A. Feed a bight of rope through the anchor. Be sure you are securely clipped into the anchor first! Use TWO quick draws. B. Tie a figure eight knot that will reach your harness into the bight of rope. C. Clip the figure eight knot into a LOCKING carabiner attached to your harness. D. Untie the rope from your harness, and you are ready to lower.

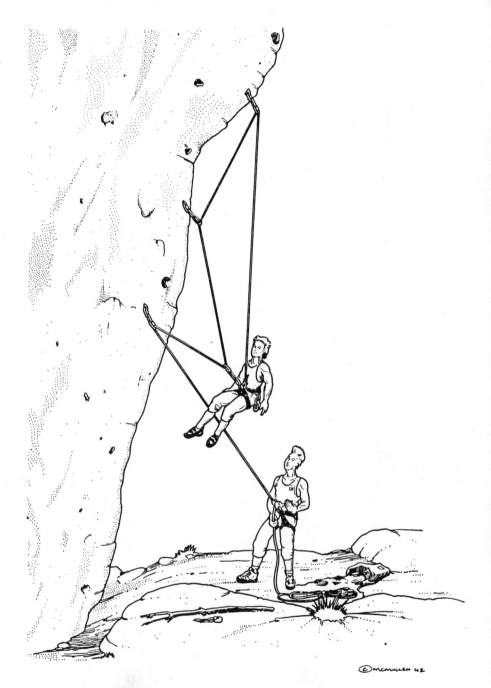

**Figure 4-10**  This is a method you can use to leave the rope clipped into a high
point (or piece of protection). Works very well for avoiding repeated
stick clips.

## Cleaning a Pitch

Cleaning the gear from of a modern bolted route is usually not a problem. If you are climbing using clean protection in cracks, the removal of such gear is an acquired skill. When you are cleaning this type of protection, it's important to bring a cleaning tool. There are several different types. Some have a feature that will aid in the removal of stubborn SLCDs and TCUs.

The problem of hard-to-remove gear is not the fault of the following climber, usually. It is more often the fault of an overexcited leader who has not had much experience placing protection. Nuts should be slotted, then gently tugged to set. SLCDs do not have to be set deep in a crack to be effective and safe. As a leader, it is your responsibility to place gear in such a way as to be easily removed by your partner. Often a piece of gear that is placed in desperation will probably be hard to get out, although a leader should not hesitate to over-place a piece of protection if getting it in fast is critical or necessary to prevent a bad fall.

## Logistics for Multipitch Routes

One important skill for multipitch routes is the belay exchange. Where a climber leads a pitch and then gives the next lead to a partner, a few tactics lend to the process. The climber that is following a pitch, cleaning the route, will organize the gear along the way to facilitate the process of passing quickly and with the least amount of gear-sorting or confusion. There will be a piece of protection above the belay already clipped by the first leader so that the new leader now can proceed quickly upward into the next pitch.

Long free climbing routes require organization and preparation for weather and a possible bivouac.

**Figure 4-11**  Using a quick draw, attached to your harness and connected to the
rope which runs up and through the quick draws on a route, will
enable you to stay close enough to the wall to clean it. BE VERY
CAREFUL when unclipping from the last (or first) piece of
protection. You will swing backwards!

# 5. BODY MAINTENANCE AND TRAINING

High and sustained achievement demands
the concentration of life.
— *Anatole France*

The underlying goal of all climbers is personal excellence. This means that you do whatever you can to get stronger, smoother, more confident, and closer to the top of the grade scale. Some climbers who are reading this book will eventually be the best in the world. Some climbers with equal drive and potential will have short and disappointing careers. The one thing most likely to divide these two groups is physical injury. It is far more important to avoid injury than to become heinously strong. A race car is only impressive until its engine blows, at which point, a beat-to-hell '71 pickup that runs on five cylinders is superior.

It's very important to stretch and warm up effectively before climbing or training. But often this is not enough to avoid strains in your fingers, wrists, or elbows. If you are feeling discomfort or are certain you are going to be climbing hard on a given day, it is advisable to tape sensitive areas (most notably the fingers).

## Taping
Taping is not a method of relieving pain that already exists.

If you are having problems, give your body a rest. A full rest is usually the best way to recover from strains or other injuries.

### Fingers

The index and middle finger are the strongest and most often used. It is wise to tape them if you plan to climb steep or overhanging pocketed climbs. Pocketed routes are very hard on tendons, and a small amount of tape and a good warm-up can save you from a lot of pain. They should be taped between the first and second knuckles and between the second and third. If properly done, the tape will not interfere with the flexibility of the joints but will give support to the sensitive tendons in the fingers. If you will be using other fingers on small mono moves, tape those fingers as well.

Don't hesitate to tape your ring finger every time you climb, including training. This is the finger that is most easily injured.

### Wrists

If you need more wrist support, wrap cloth tape around your wrists a couple of times.

### Elbows

Many climbers seem to suffer some sort of elbow pain. The problem stems from improper training or climbing hard without balancing the joint. By balance we mean that it is important to train the entire joint. Without this type of training the muscles that you use for climbing are not supported properly.

If you have neglected training the joint properly and are suffering from elbow pain, it is critical that you some time off. Start out by taking a break from climbing for a couple of weeks or a month. If you continue to climb, it will only get worse. Take the time off! In two weeks you can start to do light workouts. Spend some time in the gym doing exercises that will balance the joint. Work your way back to health. It will take some time but you will be stronger when you get back to full power.

Taping an elbow after injury is not advisable. This may allow you to climb, but the injury may not heal properly and may become chronic.

### *Taping Hands for Crack Climbing and to Prevent Other Injuries*

Difficult crack climbing can tear up your hands. The damage is usually caused by poor technique but occasionally is due to the sharp texture of some types of rock. Taping hands for crack climbing on such abrasive rock will cause you to lose a certain amount of flexibility or feeling and may restrict your ability on face climbing you might encounter on a route. I suggest that you don't tape unless you have to.

### *Taping techniques*

There are many different techniques for taping hands; it seems everybody does it differently. Crack gloves, such as Spider Mitts, can save a lot of tape.

The common method of taping hands is to start between your thumb and index finger, wrapping the tape around your palm two or three times, making sure to cover your knuckles, then wrapping the tape around your wrist a time or two. Be sure to move your wrist while taping so you don't tape the flexibility out of it.

If you need extra sticking power for the tape, you can use a spray called Tuffskin.

## Finger Care

If you climb four or more days a week, you're going to find that your fingers will take a lot of abuse. Crimpers are especially hard on the tips of fingers, and pockets will wreck your fingers if you fail to warm up properly. Be careful anywhere a hold isolates a finger.

The most important factor in preventing finger injuries is proper warm-up. We can't stress this enough. Warm up! The harder you plan to climb, the longer you should warm up.

Shredded tips are hard to prevent, and even harder to ignore. There are not many things that hurt more than a gash in your fingertip. You might find that training on artificial holds will help. They're pretty rough and help develop fingertip calluses.

## How to Handle Pain and What to Do to Prevent It

Pain is difficult to avoid. If you climb, you know pain. You probably know many manifestations of it. For instance, the pain you feel in your feet from those ultra-tight shoes. And the day after a hard session of pocket pulling.

Most pain is caused by overuse or improper training. It is important to use some self-control (what's that?). If you are not climbing regularly, you need to take it easy out there. Weekend trips are great, but if you only climb once a month don't do too many routes or tackle too much difficulty. Be sure to warm up on a finger board or some easy routes before you jump on the big one. For those who climb four or more days a week, it is important to take rest days. Rest days allow your body to recover and heal. Set a schedule and stick to it. A good schedule is to climb and train hard, two days, say, then rest.

Always give your body some time to recover from a workout. Your muscles grow during this period, and you will be stronger on climbing days if you give yourself sufficient time to recover.

Small amounts of aspirin help relieve finger burn from training on artificial hold (or ibuprofen, for minor muscle pain and sore joints).

Diet is a large part of the healing process. If you feed your muscles the right types of nutrients, they will recover faster. And you will have less pain. Always drink plenty of fluids!

## Diet for the Weight-Conscious Climber

Climbers work hard to climb routes at the high end of the grade scale. Weight to strength ratio is a critical factor, although today's climbers are extremely weight-loss oriented (often to the loss of strength). It is generally true that reducing body fat will make a tremendous difference in performance. Yet muscle weighs more than fat. So how does one keep light without sacrificing strength? By reducing the amount of fatty foods you eat (don't you love those chocolate chip cookies!?) your weight will be much easier to control.

Unfortunately, maintaining a good diet will not take off the fat. A regular fitness program will aid in losing unwanted body fat, and the process will be sped up considerably by thirty to sixty minutes of aerobic exercise a day.

It is relatively easy to improve your climbing ability at first, but it gets increasingly harder as you peak. This is when diet and training begin to be much more important.

Climbers need to build strong muscles that are well balanced. Climbers, unlike body builders, must develop their bodies for use -not for show. It is important to build a sufficient amount of muscle so that you will be able to have the power to climb. Power is the key word. If you think that losing weight alone will make you a better climber, you will be greatly disappointed when you find that you are lacking the power you need to climb really hard. It is important to keep body fat low, but being light will help only if you develop the strength to go with it.

Eat well. Foods such as whole wheat bread or bagels, egg whites, fruit, oatmeal or Metabolol with high-fiber cereal, and skim milk are some suggestions for breakfast.

For lunch try low-fat fish, no-fat crackers, rice with veggies, veggie sandwiches, steamed vegetables, pasta dishes, or pasta salads. Be creative!

Your afternoon (or early evening) meal should be slightly smaller than lunch. Baked or boiled potatoes with veggies, pasta dishes, steamed fresh, or frozen vegetables, lean meat, low-fat fish or chicken (without skin!) are a few suggestions.

Consuming dairy products should be kept to a minimum. Use no-fat skim milk or tofu drinks for your breakfast foods. There are several varieties of low fat cheese that will enhance the taste of sandwiches and other dishes.

Lean meat is an excellent source of protein. Meat from wild game is exceptionally lean and much healthier than many forms of store-bought meats.

You need not sacrifice taste because you are dieting. There are many great recipes and a good number of cookbooks especially written for the athlete.

### When to Eat on Off Days

When you eat is as important as what you eat. On rest days, it is better to eat large meals in the morning. Have a medium-sized meal for lunch and then very little for dinner. Refrain from eating later than nine o'clock. Meals eaten late digest slowly, making it difficult to get a restful sleep. If you eat late, do some type of physical activity to aid in digesting these foods.

### On Days

On climbing days, you should eat small meals or snacks to keep your energy level balanced. Less energy will be expended digesting food. Try a bowl of Metabolol with grape nuts and no-fat skim milk. Cytobars will help you maintain energy throughout the day. Drink plenty of water!

### Diet Supplements

*Food Bars*

Cytobar is one bar proven effective through university studies. Food bars contain a large percentage of vitamins, minerals, and essential amino acids your body needs daily. They contain little fat (less than two grams per bar) and no cholesterol. Food bars are used by many climbers because they are easy to carry.

Another Champion Nutrition product, Metabolol II is a complete food product and tastes great! Used wisely, along with a balanced diet, Metabolol will assist you in building and maintaining  strength and energy. All Champion Nutrition products have been tested through university studies and are proven effective. Other supplements can be beneficial to training. If you believe you need them, get the advice of a nutritionist.

## Fluids

Water helps the body produce and use fuel more efficiently. A lack of water in your body can cause it to take needed fluid from tendons and joints. If you are not drinking enough water, your body will actually hold more water to make up for the deficiency. Always drink plenty of water throughout the day, especially if you are trying to control your weight. Dehydration affects coordination, power, and endurance-leaving you hanging when you need complete control.

Using a proven athletic drink such as Cytomax (mixed with water) will give you more energy than will plain water. Cytomax contains components that are used efficiently by your body. These components aid in lowering lactic acid levels for less burning and cramping during training. Cytomax contains electrolytes, no sucrose, and just a small amount of sodium. You will be able to maintain peak level longer, allowing you to train and climb harder.

Your body needs a source of carbohydrates about every ninety minutes during a hard session of training or climbing. A source supplying about twenty-five grams ingested every half an hour will help maintain your energy level. Most sport drinks contain 5 to 10 percent carbohydrate. A cup and a half every half hour should supply the necessary amount of carbos you will need.

### Caffeine

Swilling large quantities of coffee before climbing is a weakness of many climbers. One problem with this is that by the time you get to the climbing the energy surge caused by the caffeine is gone, doing you absolutely no good!

## Training

There comes a time in every climbing career when mileage and motivation alone fail to add up to measurable improvement. When an improvement curve flattens out, a carefully applied training program will often set the stage for further breakthroughs. A certain amount of gym work will also help stave off the ever-present specter of injury. The most important aspect of training is to focus; define your objective and never waver in its pursuit. Training for its own sake is a waste of critical energy. Always train for a tangible goal such as a big wall, a route, a known move, a certain hand position. Define, pursue relentlessly, realize, and then define again.

Serious climbers push themselves to their absolute limits. To do so requires a great amount of dedication and commitment both physically and mentally.

Physically, climbers must be in top shape to climb many of today's modern free climbs. To get in shape, climbers pursue rigorous training schedules which include working out at a climbing gym, a low-fat diet, and good aerobic exercise, such as road, trail, or stair running.

Mental training takes the form of meditation, and visualization, and is important preparation for climbs that require many technical moves that must be memorized.

As a beginner, you will find that it is not as important to train for climbing as it is to gain experience climbing routes that are within your ability. Through this experience you can target your weaknesses and plan a training program. This philosophy is important to advanced climbers as well. For example, if you find you are strong on climbs that require intricate footwork and use of small edges (crimpers) but you lack power when climbing overhanging routes with large holds, you should design your workouts in such a way that you stress building power in the muscles that will be needed to climb overhangs.

A common mistake in training is overtraining parts of your body that are already strong and ignoring the parts that need the most work. The amount of training you need to do to improve your strength for climbing can be seen in the following graph.

What you see in the graph is that the amount of effort put into training is rewarded by an equal amount of improvement up to a point where it begins to taper off. At this point, you'll find progress to be more difficult. It takes much longer to make any substantial improvement. When improvement begins to taper off, you have to reevaluate your training and develop a new plan.

Peaks occur differently for different climbers. Some people are capable of progressing easily to 5.9, others to 5.13. Whatever your peak seems to be, you will know when you hit it. And you should know that you can, if you want to, surpass that.

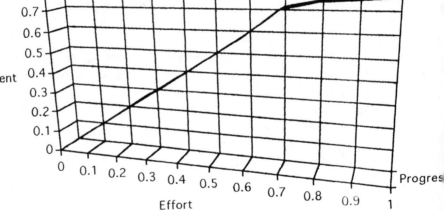

**Figure 5-1**    Progress graph

You will find numerous training programs, some of which will  assist you better than others in getting into shape for climbing. Training programs should be used as a guide and modified to your personal needs. If you are trying to follow the recommendations of another climber, you will probably find that you need to modify the routine to fit your body's requirements. Climbing demands total physical conditioning. It is important to build strength but not to build mass.

### *Warming up and Stretching*

Flexibility will aid your climbing. A regular stretching session at home (or wherever) will improve your flexibility. Your stretching routine outside of climbing can be combined with the usual warm-ups before climbing.

Activities such as jumping rope, easy running, biking, rowing, or stair machines are good activities you can pursue in addition to climbing that will contribute to climbing and to your aerobic fitness.

It is important that your fingers be warmed up too. When you are in the gym, warm them up by walking along an overhanging wall-reaching from one hold to the next. Don't do long reaches. Pinch or grip each hold, using a variety of hand positions. Do not hang from the holds, just grab as many as you can from the ground. You will feel your hands begin to warm up. If you want to warm them up more, go to the finger board and do some hangs with an open grip. Do not use a cling grip or do pull ups on small holds. When ready to climb, do a couple of warm up routes before you attempt to do anything hard. Build slowly to higher difficulties. Then crank until the lights go out!

### *Free Weight Training*

Beginners and experts can use free weights to balance the training of different areas of the body. Women who are starting to climb will find that free weight training is a good way to build muscle in areas where they may be lacking power. It's a lot of fun too! You can develop muscles quickly if you are disciplined and stick to a good workout routine. It is important, however, that as you build those weak areas you do not overdo it. Remember also that you should be working out to build balance and power-not mass.

Free weight training is not as simple as picking up weights. There is a technique and method for each exercise. Learn from someone who has experience. You can find many good books on weight training, and usually a sport center will provide instructors.

### Weight Machines
A close relative of the free weight, weight machines allow you to isolate specific muscle groups with a large amount of control. They enable you to work on only those muscles that need to be built to improve the balance of a joint. For example, if you are doing a lot of pull ups to build your biceps, you should do an equal number of tricep pull downs to balance the training. Weight machines are excellent for this purpose.

### Finger Boards
Doing a disciplined workout on the finger board will help your climbing immensely. Fingers are best strengthened by doing open handed hangs from various holds, without doing pull-ups. If you are doing pull-ups, which tend more to build arm strength than finger strength, you should use the biggest holds on the board.

### Rock Gyms
There are many new rock gyms popping up around the United States. They give the beginner a safe, enjoyable introduction to climbing and an opportunity to observe and learn from climbers that already have developed skills. Using a gym can improve your climbing skills immensely. Rock gyms that are large enough to include lead routes are great fun, especially on rainy days!

If you are interested in getting involved in competition, you should probably be climbing in a gym. Plastic holds are quite different than the natural rock and take some practice to get used to. Most climbing competitions are held in gyms. By working out at a gym or being a member, you will get information you need to break into the sport.

### Home Gyms
Small but efficiently designed gyms can be constructed in your garage or in a storage area. Important features to add to

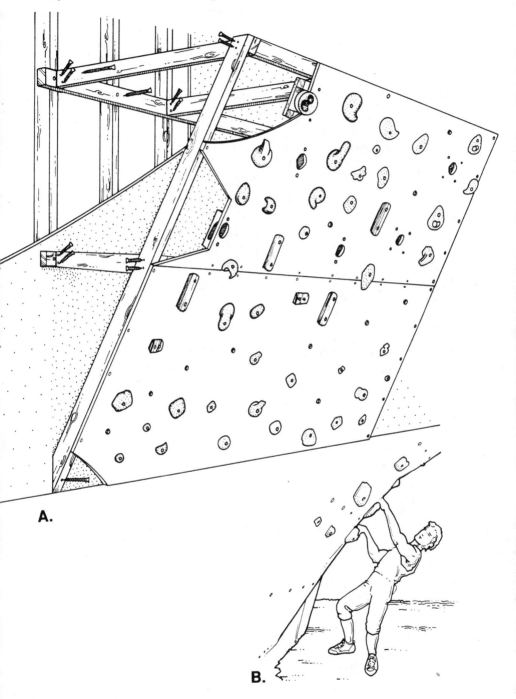

**Figure 5-12** A. Basic climbing wall construction. The steeper the structure, the harder the workout. B. Warm up before a hard workout!

your home gym are a good overhanging bouldering area, a roof, and walls that are slightly over 90 degrees. When building your gym, you should design the climbing to improve your weaknesses or to develop simulators for the type of climbing that you are attempting to do.

### Overhang Training

An overhanging training surface should have as many holds on it as it will hold. If the holds are numbered or named, you will be able to develop specific problems to work on. Pad the area below the overhang well . . . I mean really well. You want to be able to give every problem 100 percent effort.

The most important benefit of having a home gym is that it is always near when you want to train. If you do not have room for a home gym, the best things you can do to improve your strength are: climb, go bouldering, do finger board workouts, and do rolling hand curls.

## What Will Work Best for You?

Every climber I have ever known has had his or her preferred maintenance and training routine and diet. It is important to customize your routines and diet to fit your needs. Important things to remember are:
- Have a well balanced diet
- Drink plenty of fluids
- Train for muscular balance
- Concentrate on improving your weaknesses, not your strengths
- Work hard but do not overtrain
- Protect vulnerable areas such as hands and fingers
- If you injure yourself, rest and build your strength back gradually
- Use training equipment safely
- Most importantly, get out on the rock and find out if it's working!

# 6. Competitive Sport Climbing

Organized competitions are a facet of the sport that each climber must make up his or her own mind about. Some climbers abhor them and some see them as the only reason to live. The important thing is not to be forced into them by peer pressure or be forced out of them by fear of failure. You only have so many climbing days, and it is a crime to waste even one doing something you don't love to do. Whether it is a local fun comp or a World Cup worth thousands, participate because you want to and for no other reason. Don't forget to enjoy yourself!

The term "sport climbing" was coined in Europe in the mid-1980's and refers to competitive climbing or climbing of routes that have permanent bolts placed for protection.

Authors' Note: We think that the term "sport" climbing best describes indoor climbing only. There are too many uncontrollable aspects involved in climbing outdoors to call it sport; we therefore refer to bolt-protected routes that are outdoors simply as bolt-protected rock climbs

## The Arena

Competitions were originally held on real rock. This didn't go over too well for several reasons. Holds were created or chiseled into the rock, and bolts were added to cliffs on routes that already existed . . . not too cool! Because of environmental impact and inability to control the difficulty of the climbing, competitions have been held with more success on indoor artificial climbing structures. In the beginning, most of the structures for climbing competitions were not permanent. Their design was made up of modular towers that could be arranged in numerous configurations for different events. Several types of surface panels were used, some very realistic and others abstract. These large structures are still used for most of the big international competitions and will probably be the type of wall used if sport climbing becomes an Olympic event.

Due to the increasing number of rock gyms popping up around the world, more and more events are being held on a local level.

Sport climbing is a relatively young sport in the United States, and competitions still have varying degrees of organization. Usually for an event to be considered world class, it must be sanctioned by the UIAA. Anyone can compete in a sanctioned event. But in order for your points to be included in the national ranking system, you must be a member of the American Sport Climbers Federation (ASCF).

The ASCF is a member of the Comité Internationale de Competition d'Escalade (CICE). This committee is responsible for organizing all of the national teams and directing the sport so that it will become eligible as an Olympic sport. The CICE is a branch of the UIAA.

The ASCF is responsible for the approval of events that it believes are important in the development of the sport in the United States. Sanctioned events are intended to bring climbers that may be qualified as national team members. In order for you to become a member of the U.S. Climbing Team, you must accumulate points in sanctioned events.

## The U.S. Climbing Team

The national team of the United States is made up of ASCF members who have proven through sanctioned events that they are the best representatives of the United States to compete in events at the international level. The team consists of two women and three men who compete in each international event. The team is backed by a group of alternate climbers (all nationally ranked ASCF members).

## Competitive Levels

Although elite competitions and competitors are the most well known, there are competitions held that include the beginner and intermediate as well. Fun Comps are designed for the enjoyment of all and involve classes for everyone. If you have your sights set on becoming a member of the national team, or if you just enjoy competition, there is an event for you. Common divisions for these competitors are:

### Children's Levels

Jr. for competitors under a specified age

### Adult

Novice class-ability level below 5.10
Intermediate class-ability level between 5.10 and 5.11+
Advanced class-ability level above 5.12 but not exceeding 5.13
Open class-a class which allows climbers to attempt to enter
    the elite class.

### Expert

Competitors who climb at the professional level are classified as Elite, Expert, or Masters. Climbers entering this class must generally be able to on-sight 5.12. This requirement will go up in the future as climbers continue to improve.

Since all competitions are not organized by one governing organization, the titles of these divisions may vary (depending on the location of the event).

## Format

Competitive sport climbing can be practiced in many different formats. Many of the most prestigious competitions use only the on-sight format. This tests the ability of the climber on an unknown course. The winner of the event is who reaches the highest point on the course.

Some competitions are now including a redpoint format, allowing the climbers to work on a course for a specified number of tries before attempting to climb it without falling.

Competitions in speed climbing have existed for many years. They were originally the conception of a Russian organization in the 1970's. The first Americans to compete in a speed climbing competition in the U.S.S.R., Todd Skinner, Beth Wald, Russ Clune, and Dan Michael, reported that "climbing fast made little sense!" Speed climbing, however, expresses a different kind of talent than usual and continues to be an interesting event that shares a place in most climbing competitions. It is especially exciting to watch as a spectator.

There are several other formats for climbing competitions. Most are designed for fun, nonsanctioned competitions, and are set up primarily to give the competitors an enjoyable experience.

## Behind the Scenes

There are many people involved in the organization of a climbing competition. All are responsible for specific tasks, and their cooperation is what makes competitions enjoyable (or hellish!). Since there are still many competitions not ASCF-sanctioned, the rules and organization of events may vary. All ASCF-sanctioned events must be judged and run according to UIAA rules.

### Course setting

A climbing competition could not be held if there were no routes to climb. The climbing routes or courses are set by the course setters. Creativity, climbing experience, and an extensive understanding of rope management are critical in setting an interesting course for the competitors. Course setters must have a good deal of real rock climbing experience to set routes that are of the exact rating needed for a specific class. This is a difficult task, since a route may favor the taller climber . . . or favor one type of climber.

### Forerunners

A forerunner is a person licensed by the UIAA to set routes and check other aspects of a competition route prior to the event. Forerunners are responsible for setting all routes that are UIAA sanctioned. They are responsible for checking the safety of the route, including the equipment used and the safety of the entire protection system. They also must confirm that the route is of the difficulty required by the competition level. Becoming a forerunner involves taking a special instructional course and being tested by a UIAA-certified forerunning instructor. The forerunner certification course is very difficult and requires one to climb routes that are at the highest level of difficulty.

### *Judges and Juries*

The organization of judges consists of the president of the jury, referees for each category, the heat judges (one each for men's & women's heats), and the route jury. The route jury is led by the chief route judge. He is assisted by the technical judges (such as the measurers, time keepers, belayers, and video judges). One jury is responsible for an individual route in each round of competition if a competitor wishes to protest or appeal a situation, the judgment will be made by an impartial group rather than by an individual.

### *Rules*

Events not sanctioned by the ASCF or the UIAA will have varying rules you will have to follow. If you are interested in a complete list of UIAA Regulations Governing Climbing Competitions, I recommend you contact the ASCF.

The rules for a ASCF/UIAA–sanctioned climbing competition are fairly complex and should be studied carefully by any climber seriously considering becoming a professional. The rules for an event are designed according to the competition format. The rules for an on-sight format will be different from those for a redpoint format. This is why it is important to study all of the rules before entering a competition. Always attend competition meetings prior to the event.

Never assume that you know the rules governing an event. At the 1989 Snowbird International Climbing Championships, many of the competitors did not attend the precompetition competitors' meeting. Some of the best climbers in the world fell off the starting moves of the semi-finals route because they did not know where the course boundaries were, something they would have known had they attended the meeting.

## Sport Climbing Organizations in the United States

The official organization for competitive climbing in the United States is the American Sport Climbers Federation, 125 West 96th Street Suite #1D, New York, NY 10025. Membership for individuals is $25.00 at this time.

## Getting Involved in Sport Climbing Competition

If you are interested in competing, it is as easy as going to the nearest rock gym and entering. Many gyms offer fun competitions for those who are not interested in becoming professional competitors. There are a lot of fun outdoor events you can compete in also, such as bouldering competitions. Climbers in Phoenix have had organized bouldering competitions for a number of years in their area. They are really fun! If you've never been to one to compete, you should at least go as a spectator. The parties afterward are legendary.

If, however, you are seriously thinking of becoming a professional, first join the ASCF. To be nationally ranked, you will have to compete in as many sanctioned events as are required by the ASCF to acquire the necessary amount of points. More information will be provided to you upon joining. The location of events and dates they are to be held are found in the mainstream climbing magazines.

# 7. New Routes and Ethics

Style is the hallmark of
a temperament stamped upon
the material at hand.
— *Andre Maurois*

Establishing and naming a new route is the most satisfying milestone of a career for many climbers. Some see it as a path to fame, since it is an accomplishment literally written in stone. Others see it as a manifestation of creativity and feel an artist's pride. A route is often considered a reflection of its author. For this reason and many others, the utmost care should be taken by the first ascentionist. As you ponder a first ascent, keep future climbers in mind. If you're a 5.13 climber, don't establish a death runout on a 5.7 face. In so doing, you steal the route from future 5.6 and 5.7 climbers. If you can't quite make a move, don't chop a four-finger-mondo-jug so you can do it that day. In doing so you steal the route from everybody who will ever be better than you. If you must put bolts in a climb, then you must do a perfect job. A perfectly bolted 5.11 will be a joy for advanced climbers and an aspiration for beginners. Each route should be a credit to the locals in that area.

Discussion is an exchange
of knowledge,
argument an exchange
of ignorance.

— *Robert Quillen*

## Communication

Years ago, you could go to any climbing area and easily find
unclimbed routes. These days it's not as easy to find a line that
hasn't been climbed. Sometimes it is difficult to tell if a route
has been established unless it bears permanent anchors such as
bolts or fixed pins. Many unknowing climbers have bolted rock
that was climbed without bolts by earlier climbers. If you're
looking at a crack, there's a good chance it has been done.

If you see a feature that you're interested in climbing, it's
best to ask fellow climbers if the line has been climbed. Be
patient-get good information from a reliable source. Jumping
the gun may get you into trouble with other climbers,
especially if you place permanent anchors on a route that has
been climbed using clean protection. Use discretion if you plan
on putting a route up in an area that still adheres to traditional
ethics. It's often possible to get the locals' support if you try.

Modern climbers are far better off searching out new
climbing areas where they can establish routes without having
to deal with established localized traditional ethics. Climbers
today are finding many new cliffs that lend themselves to the
"modern" method.

When you've preplaced protection on a route, it is important
to let others know that you are working on the route.
Otherwise, if no one knows you are active on a route, you may
find all your gear missing when you come back to work on the
project at a later date. Don't take it for granted that if you leave
gear it will be there when you return. Let locals know where
and what you're working on so they can help you keep an eye
on the project and any equipment left on it.

It's a good idea to mark a route you're working on if you do
not want others to attempt climbing it before you finish. An
easy way to do this is to mark the first bolt in some way. A red
shoestring or bright piece of tape works well. This method is
based purely on honor. If someone comes to you someday

saying that they did it before you, don't be surprised. This is one of the drawbacks of preplacing gear on a route.

If a climb is taking a long time to complete or redpoint, you may want to consider opening it to the attempts of others. This choice is up to you, so it's better to pick your best friend and give him a shot at it before others come along and snag the redpoint behind your back. If you've been working on a climb for more than a year and are not active on it, it's a good idea to let others try it.

> The creative process is not limited
> to the arts and to thought;
> it is wide as life.
> — *Brewster Ghiselin*

## Picking a line

Choosing the line is the most creative aspect of putting up a new route. It can happen suddenly or can take a number of years to visualize. Crack climbs are generally a little easier to spot than difficult face climbs and require less route-finding creativity.

When visualizing the line of a face route, it is often impossible to plot the course of the route until you actually attempt to climb it. A face climb may require some experimenting before a route can be firmly established.

If possible, set up a top rope without placing any permanent anchors, using a tree, clean protection, or anchors from another route. Do not place any permanent anchors until the line is firmly established. This will prevent the placement of unnecessary bolts if the route is not climbable or takes a different direction than you thought it would.

### Working the Route

If the route you are trying to establish exceeds your limit, you may have to work on it for some time before you can climb it. There are numerous top rope techniques that enable you to safely work on a route.

Don't place bolts on a route before you can climb it, unless you have a lot of experience and are absolutely sure that the placements are necessary and will be in the right place.

### *Cleaning the Route*

Cleaning loose rock from a new route is often necessary whether you are climbing traditionally or using top-down methods. Use discretion when cleaning. You may later regret removing any feature, and it may not be possible to replace a feature once it is removed. If cleaning a route, always check below for people who may be climbing nearby. Warn them of the falling rock. Altering the rock is a questionable tactic, and if you choose to follow this path you will probably pick up some bad karma along the trail.

> Anyone who plunges into infinity,
> in both time and space,
> needs fixed points, otherwise
> his movement is indistinguishable
> from standing still.
>
> — *M. C. Escher*

## To Bolt or Not to Bolt?

The fact that bolts are "in style" in many communities of thought does not mean that their use should be flagrant. Careful consideration should be given to every bolt placement. If you have climbed a route on top rope and believe you should place fixed protection, here are some things you should consider:

1. What are the ethics of the area in which you are climbing? It is not advisable to bolt in an area that honors traditional ethics; that is, unless you get the permission of the local climbers.

2. Will the placement of permanent anchors cause property owners or others to be upset or angry, and is it worth upsetting them? Many conflicts of interest can be avoided with good communication.

3. The placement of bolts should be permanent. If they are removed or vandalized, they will cause a permanent scar on the rock. It is best not to just assume that it is okay to bolt in any area. You must decide if you want to be involved in the issues this action will cause.

4. Bolting a climb in an area that lends itself to traditional ethics is something that should be thought over carefully. It can cause serious repercussions to you and others. Whole climbing areas have been closed due to the

carelessness of a few climbers. Try to avoid these circumstances by communicating with not only local climbers but with any agency that may be involved with the property you are climbing on.

### *Placing Top Anchors*

Placement of rappel anchors has been common on many routes for years. The placement of rappel anchors on modern routes has, however, been handled differently. Many modern climbs do not end on the top of the rock; they instead end at the top of a face. This means anchors are sometimes placed at the end of a face climb, not on top of the rock. They can be difficult to get to if you are not familiar with the placement of clean climbing gear such as nuts or SLCDs and with advanced rappel techniques.

When placing the top anchors on a new route, consider how others are going to get to them. Place them in a position easily accessible. Use large bolts for top anchors and a chain or special

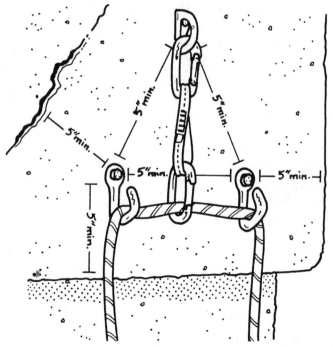

**Figure 7-1**    Anchors should be placed at least one foot apart as well as away from cracks or edges. Always back up open cold shuts with a standard bolt and hanger. Use 1/2 inch bolts at belays if possible.

rappel bolt hangers. Cold shuts that are not welded are used on some routes and should be backed up by a standard bolt. Often they are not: use them at your own risk. There are some welded cold shuts that are okay (we wish they would make them bigger).

### Bolting a Face

When you have decided to bolt a face, you should give serious consideration to the type of bolt you use. There are many types of bolts, but not all are strong enough to be used for climbing anchors. The type we recommend in all rock is the solid head sleeve bolt, the bigger the better. If you're going to place it, make it bomber!

Again the Hilti-HSL, Rawl bolt, and the Petzl Coeurgoujon are the best all-around bolts as of this edition. If you are placing anchors into soft rock, we recommend glue-in bolts such as the Chem-stud or Petzl Ring or Collinox used with glue. Glue-in bolts are good for all types of rock but are best for soft rock.

For hard rock, an excellent choice is the Petzl long-life nail drive bolt.

Always use the beefiest, best hanger you can get. Please! Don't use homemade hangers! These things are u-g-l-y! They are never as well made as a production bolt and receive no testing. Who wants to clip these darn things? It's a horrible sight to see a beautiful route degraded by ugly hangers.

### Drills

Always use a power drill to place bolts on modern routes. The only exception is if you are in an area that has banned the use of power drills and you are forced to use a hand-held percussion drill. If you have to hand drill, take your time. Make the hole as perfect as possible.

Power drills make the cleanest, fastest, and most perfect hole for the placement of a bolt. They also make the placement stronger. There are two types of power drills: battery-powered or gas-powered. If you are working in remote areas, the gas-powered drill is preferable. You will have to carry fuel, but it is cheaper than buying batteries.

For a local area, you can use a battery-powered drill. Battery life will vary depending on the type of drill you have. A Bosch Bulldog will drill approximately eight holes in medium to hard

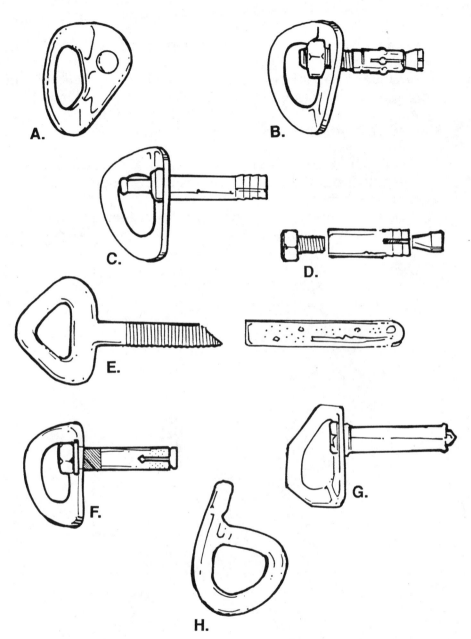

Figure 7-2    A. A PETZL hanger. A good example of the type of hanger that
should be used on all modern routes. B. PETZL Coeurgoujon solid
head sleeve bolt with hanger. C. PETZL long life nail drive bolt. D. A
PETZL self drive bolt. E. A PETZL ring bolt and glue capsule. F. A
RAWL solid head sleeve bolt. G. A STARDRYVN nail drive bolt. H. A
welded GOLDSHUT cold shut.

dolomite before re-charging. If you need more power, you can buy an extra battery or two.

Using a power drill is relatively simple on less than vertical or vertical rock. It can, however, be tricky if you are working on overhanging rock or a roof. It's good to have some experience in aid climbing in this situation, otherwise you can get into trouble.

Some routes are so overhanging that it is actually easier to place bolts from the ground up. Again this requires some aid climbing experience.

Bolts are meant as permanent protection. Careful consideration should be given to every placement. Don't get in a hurry!

> Egotism is the anesthetic that
> dulls the pain of stupidity.
> > — *Frank Leaky*

# 8. MODERN CLIMBING AREAS

Rudeness is the weak man's
imitation of strength.
— *Eric Hoffer*

Almost every state has climbable rock, and more is being discovered every year. Half of the beauty of this sport is that it gives you a reason to hit the road in search of rock that you haven't touched. Each area is unique, and many obscure destinations have a charm that the famous areas lose. Travel widely, keep an open mind and be friendly to visitors in your home areas.

This chapter is dedicated to those climbers out there who are pushing the limits of modern free climbing. We know how much work goes into putting up new routes (and the costs involved), and that you're not always rewarded by the climbers that come along after you (you know, the youngsters that are flashing your routes now). We would like to recognize a number of these new areas, and some that are not so new.

There are many climbing areas in the United States. Those that are not listed here most certainly have their own guidebooks that detail their history.

In the following pages are the location of and a little info on some of our favorite climbing areas. This is not meant as a guide substitute. You will have to search out information from the areas' locals or read their guides. Maps of site locations can be found in Appendix A.

# Alabama

### *Yellow Creek Falls*

Located in northeastern Alabama, Yellow Creek Falls may be the finest climbing area in the state. The routes are long, steep, and the sandstone superb. Routes tend to be difficult, but there are climbs suited to beginner or intermediate. The beauty of the area alone makes it worth visiting. You can stock up on food and other supplies in the nearby towns of Centre or Leesburg. Camping is limited in the immediate area but can be found near Sandrock, fifteen minutes away. You can climb at Yellow Creek year 'round, but the best seasons are fall and winter.

### *Sandrock*

Sandrock is one of the most popular climbing areas in Alabama and offers a wide variety of routes at various levels of difficulty. The climbing is located near the small town of Centre, Alabama. Supplies can be obtained in the towns of Leesburg and Centre-both of which offer hotels, stores, and restaurants. The climbing is on sandstone, with traditional as well as bolt-protected climbs. Unfortunately the area has been somewhat abused and is not as beautiful as it once was. The best seasons for climbing are fall and winter, but climbing is possible year 'round. Camping is available but is primitive. Water is not available at the area.

# Arizona

### *Virgin River Gorge "VR"*

The Virgin River Gorge is located in the far northwest corner of Arizona, approximately twenty minutes south of St. George, Utah. This modern climbing area is very near a major highway (I-15) and is somewhat loud and obnoxious in terms of aesthetics. Nevertheless the climbing is good, and the locals who are developing the area will tell you it is well worth a visit-especially if you are interested in steep (overhanging) bolt-protected climbing. The routes are on limestone and are moderate to difficult. Parking is available at pullouts below the cliffs. Camping areas are located a few miles north. The Virgin River Gorge Recreational area has campsites for a fee, and free camping can be found on Blackrock road. Water is found at the V.R.G. Recreation area also. You will have to go to St. George to purchase food, gas, or other such. The climbing season at VR is year 'round.

### Mount Lemon-Windy Point

This excellent climbing area is located approximately twenty-five minutes from Tucson, Arizona. If you are looking for climbing during the winter, this is the spot. Situated at an altitude of sixty-five hundred feet, Windy Point boasts several hundred routes ranging from 5.9 to 5.13+ on excellent rock. All supplies can be found in Tucson. Camping is available a few miles past Windy point at the Molino Basin Campground. Further information and equipment can be obtained in Tucson at South Rim Outfitters or Summit Hut.

### Superstition Mountains

These have been the backdrop for many classic western films and offer some of the finest climbing in Arizona. The approaches are a little longer than those in other areas, but to be here is worth the hike. The Superstition Wilderness is located east of Phoenix on the Superstition Freeway, approximately thirty minutes from the city. You will probably want to get the latest information from a local climber, because the area has been subject to some access problems. Climbers at Desert Mountain Sports will be more than happy to guide you in the right direction.

### Le Petit Verdon

Also known as "The Pit." This small area is a great place to stop if you are traveling through Northern Arizona. It is located about twenty minutes south of Flagstaff. Groceries and supplies can be found as you leave town. The local climbing shop is The Edge. Climbing at the Pit is on Kiabab limestone, offering pocketed face climbing. There are approximately eighty routes in the 5.9 to 5.13 range of difficulty, definitely enough to keep you happy for awhile. This is a very nice area where you can usually enjoy peace and quiet during the week. Camping is free.

### Queen Creek

This is a great spot to climb, especially on those days when the temps are raging in Phoenix. Head east from Phoenix on the superstition freeway (highway 89). About an hour of driving takes you to the little town of Superior where you can stop for supplies or have a beer at the local bar (once the longest bar in Arizona). There is not much else to do here, though. Drive on up the canyon, and you will soon find the rock. Several classics are right on the road and many more very near the road. Queen Creek has been the location of several of the now famous Phoenix Bouldering Contests. The bouldering is located approximately a mile northeast, past the canyon.

## Arkansas

### Sam's Throne

This sandstone formation, named in memory of a preacher who once gave sermons from its summit, is located in the northwest corner of Alabama. Sam's Throne has long been a popular area for Alabama and Missouri climbers. The area ethics are traditional, and bolts are only acceptable if put in on lead. The nearest town is Jasper-which has all of the supplies you may need but no climbing shop. Camping is free so far, and there are sites near the climbing area. There is an outhouse near the camping area, but water is not available. The climbing is on sandstone. Routes are seldom set up with bolts, so you will need a rack of gear and experience using it. Climbs are mostly in the moderate range, but everyone will find a challenge.

### Red Rock Point

Located near Mount Judea, this prominent bluff is visible from the west end of town. To get to the cliff, drive west on highway 374 to the top of a hill. Take a right onto a private dirt road. Follow this to its end and park. From the parking area, hike east down to the cliff. Access to this area hinges on good rapport with the land owner. Behave like kings and queens, or go with a local.

# California

### *Tuolumne Meadows*

This is probably one of the most beautiful climbing areas in the United States. Tuolumne Meadows is located high in the Sierra Nevada, in the eastern portion of Yosemite National Park, California. Climbs are on high quality granite, with knobs and crystals. The modern face climbs in Tuolumne generally ascend the overhanging sides of the area's numerous granite domes. Interested in traditional classics? Check out Pywiack Dome, Medilicott Dome, East Cottage Dome, Canopy World, Whizz Dome, or the Arena. All supplies, occasionally climbing partners, and further information can be found in Tuolumne Meadows. Camping is available in the park for a small fee. Weather is best in spring through fall (the road closes in winter).

### *Emeralds*

This sporty new area has had some rave revues. Located between Nevada City and Lake Tahoe in northern California, the Emeralds are well worth investigating. The blend of metamorphosed sedimentary and igneous rock tends to be very steep. Most of the routes in the area are at the high end of the grade scale, but there are a few climbs of interest to the intermediate. Gas and food can be found in Nevada City. If you need climbing information or gear, you will have to travel to Sacramento or Truckee.

### *Owens River Gorge*

Another outstanding modern climbing area is located in Owens River Gorge near Bishop, California. The gorge was long overlooked by traditional climbers due to the poor rock in the cracks, but a group of climbers transformed the gorge into a Mecca of outstanding bolt-protected face climbs. The rock is volcanic tuff similar to that found at Deadman's Summit. To get to the south entrance, travel north from Bishop on highway 395. Exit at Gorge Road, heading east, and follow this for 0.7 miles to a T intersection. Turn left (north) and follow this road for 3.2 miles to another T intersection. Take a right here and travel 0.25 mile to the south entrance gate and parking area. You can hike or mountain bike from the parking area as far as the area known as the DMZ. The north entrance to the gorge is 3.1 miles north of the gorge exit on highway 395. For more information on climbing at the gorge, an updated guide is available at Wilson's Eastside Sports in Bishop or at the Booky Joint in Mammoth. Camping and a hot springs are nearby.

### *Joshua Tree*

Climbing has long been a tradition in Joshua Tree National Monument. It has been the training area for many climbing pioneers over the last decade. While the majority of the climbs in J-Tree are traditional in nature, there are many new climbs considered "modern." Ratings at "JT" are what I consider traditional, meaning you better be sure you can really climb 5.12 before attempting one here. There are literally thousands of climbs at Joshua Tree. It's a good idea to get the latest copy of Randy Vogel's guide, *Joshua Tree*. Joshua Tree National Monument is located approximately an hour and a half east of Los Angeles near Twenty-nine Palms. Food, gas, and entertainment can be found in Twenty-nine Palms or the town of Joshua Tree. Camping (with water and rest rooms) is available at several locations in the park for a fee.

### *Donner Summit*

This is probably the most popular modern climbing area in northern California. Donner Summit consists of several crags, all offering superb climbing on excellent rock. Located on the east side of Donner pass, the climbing area is only minutes from Truckee (where you will find food, gas, climbing supplies, and tales of cannibalism). There are climbs at all levels of difficulty, so everyone will enjoy a visit to this beautiful area. Further information and climbing supplies can be obtained at Sierra Mountaineering in Truckee.

### *Cave Rock*

This area is on the east side of Lake Tahoe, just north of Zephyr Cove. It is home of the notorious Slayer (5.13d). There are several climbs in this large rhyolite cave worth doing. Viewing the cave alone will leave you with a case of vertigo and some spacial distortion, making the stop worthwhile. There are numerous camping areas in the vicinity, and you will find food and other supplies in South Lake Tahoe. Fall, winter, and spring are the best seasons for climbing at Cave Rock.

Some other California areas are:

*The Needles,* located north of Kernville, California. This is an outstanding group of granite domes and spires in an incredible setting.

The newly developed *New Directions Cliff, Limestone Cave* and *Sportman's Grotto* are also in the Kernville area. You will see the New Directions Cliff and the Limestone Cave on the east side of the road if you are heading north out of Kernville.

*Mickey's Beach,* which lies on the coast just north of San Francisco, offers short but fun modern climbs.

## Colorado

### *Penitente*

One of the early modern climbing areas in Colorado, Penitente is a beautiful area filled with red rock, offering steep pocketed climbing. To get to Penitente Canyon, drive north on highway 285 out of Monte Vista or South on 285 from Salida. Take the La Garita exit. Go to the town of La Garita. Food and gas are available here. From La Garita, drive west 0.5 miles. Turn left at the "Y" and follow this road for 0.8 miles. Take the next right at the wooden sign which reads "Wagon Tracks" into the mouth of the canyon.

### *Shelf Road*

Another of Colorado's early modern areas to be developed, Shelf Road has become extremely popular with the modern climber on Colorado's eastern slope as well as a climbing destination for others visiting the state. The Shelf's cliffs are limestone with edge and pocketed face climbing. Routes are generally bolt-protected and set up with excellent anchors at their belays. The area is located on a small road which connects Canon City and Cripple Creek, Colorado. Be sure to obey "no parking" notices. More information on climbing at "shelf" can be found at Mountain Chalet in Colorado Springs.

### *Rifle*

This modern climbing area is located approximately thirty-seven miles west of Glenwood Springs, and north of the small town of Rifle. The narrow canyon offers numerous routes-most of which are difficult, due to the steep nature of the rock. The canyon is filled with huge caves formed of excellent limestone. All supplies can be found in Rifle. Camping is available in Falls State Park Campground for a fee, or free camping can be found north of the canyon on BLM land. No water is available in the climbing area, so you should bring your own or get water in Rifle on the way. The best season for climbing is mid-April through October.

There are many great climbing areas around Boulder and Denver. Numerous guidebooks cover these areas.

## Idaho

### *City of Rocks*

The "City" is Idaho's premiere climbing area. To get to the City of Rocks National Reserve, take highway 27 south out of Burly, Idaho. Food and gas should be obtained in Burly. You will soon find yourself surrounded by six thousand acres of some of the finest climbing in America. City of Rocks lives up to its name. You will find routes of all levels of difficulty on the fine, high quality granite. Water as well as toilets are now available near the camping areas (which have been significantly improved). Spring, summer, and fall offer the best weather for climbing in the City.

### *Massacre*

Also known as "5.11 Heaven." Massacre Rocks is a small climbing area, but well worth a stop for a day or two of cranking steep basalt. The cliff is located forty-five minutes west of Pocatello or an hour east of City of Rocks, on I-86. The cliffs offer a full range of climbing, including pocket climbing, crack jamming, and overhangs with mondo jugs. You can climb routes from 5.9 to 5.12. The area's natural beauty is also quite impressive. With a wide variety of native wildlife, geese, hawks, pelicans, and other airborne species, you'll feel right at home whipping from a classic desperate such as Voodoo Child. You may need a raft to get across the river.

## Kentucky
### *Red River Gorge*

Ya'll should check out this place. The Red River Gorge has some of the most spectacular rock formations in the country. It is located approximately fifty miles east of Lexington, near the small town of Slade. Climbing is primarily on beautiful overhanging sandstone covered with pockets and huecos. Routes range in difficulty from 5.9 to 5.13 with the possibility of many more routes to come. The area is fairly primitive, so if you are coming from LA (or anywhere else for that matter) be prepared to deal with the local (Sneaky Hollow) gang. Camping is available three miles east of Slade on KY 15 at the Komer Ridge Campground and also at the Whittleton Campground near Hemlock Lodge. Provisions can be obtained in Slade. If you're feeling gung-ho, stop by the Military Wall on your way through the gorge. The climbing season here is typical of East-unpredictable. It can be great anytime the sun is out.

## Nevada

### *Red Rocks*

If you're looking for a great place to climb in winter, Red Rocks is the place. This massive climbing area that has long been popular has recently seen a resurgence in climbing activity. Several new areas have been developed, and many more are sure to appear. Climbs range from 5.5 to 5.13, and routes can be forty to nearly two thousand feet long. The Red Rocks area is located approximately fifteen miles west of Las Vegas. Of course in Las Vegas you will find all the gambling and nudes on ice you could possibly need. Climbing information and supplies can be found in Las Vegas at Desert Rock Sports. The climbing at Red Rocks is on sandstone which is often varnished, making it black in appearance. The multi colored rock formations in the Calico basin area are some of the most beautiful in the world. This area is the location of several new areas that are very popular with modern climbers. Camping is available at the Oak Creek Canyon campground, approximately two miles past the exit from the loop road. Water is not available at the campground, so plan accordingly.

You can climb at Red Rocks year 'round, but the summer months are very hot. If you are planning on climbing at lower altitudes, the winter weather is preferable.

### *Mount Charleston*

This new climbing area, located to the northwest of Las Vegas, promises to be an ultimate modern climbing area. The excellent limestone walls and caves have already yielded numerous high-quality routes, and the future looks good for areas such as the Boys-n-the-Hood. To get to Mount Charleston from Las Vegas, drive north on highway 95 toward Indian Springs. Take a left on highway 157 and drive past the Mount Charleston Hotel. When you reach the fork, in the road you can go straight to get to Fast Food Land, The Hood, Newland, and Pirates Cove, or you can take a right on highway 158 to a parking area below Robber's Roost. Camping is available at the trailhead which takes you to the Caribbean. It is best to stock up on food, gas, water, and other supplies in Vegas or at Indian Cove. For further information on climbing at Mount Charleston, inquire at Desert Rock Sports in Las Vegas.

## New Hampshire

New Hampshire is loaded with many great crags and cliffs that are far too numerous to describe in this book. Cliffs such as Cathedral Ledge, Humphrey's ledge, Whitehorse ledge, Cannon Cliff, Sundown Ledges, and Rumney bring to mind some of the most outstanding visions of climbing in the east. I recommend getting Ed Webster's guide, *Rock Climbs in the White Mountains of New Hampshire,* for detailed information on climbing in New Hampshire. Being a small state, it is relatively easy to get from one area to the next and to find accommodations as well as supplies in many locations. Weather is best in September and October, but you can climb from April through late fall. New Hampshire has a long tradition of climbing and is a rewarding experience-whether you're a trad or a rad.

## New York

### *The Shawangunk Range*

"The Gunks" have long been the premier climbing area of

the East. Some of the finest climbers in the world have learned to climb here, and outstanding climbers continue to develop their skills at this area. The area consists of several crags such as Skytop, The Trapps, The Near Trapps (Nears), and Milbrook. All are near the town of New Paltz which is located less than ninety miles north of Manhattan on Interstate Highway 87. The rock in the gunks is horizontally layered quartzite conglomerate. Horizontal cracks and overhangs are the main features of these formations. The number of routes, all areas included, is approximately twelve hundred, and the height of the cliffs ranges from 30 to 250 feet. Most of the routes are clean, and few have bolts. Bolting is now banned in the area. Route ratings are diverse, with routes from 5.0 to 5.13. The Shawangunks are an exceptionally beautiful area with the best seasons for climbing being spring through fall.

Gas, food, and such can be found in New Paltz. Further climbing beta and equipment can be found at Rock n' Snow. One can write and get information through the Mohonk Preserve, Mohonk Lake, New Paltz, New York 12561. Passes must be obtained to climb at all areas within the reserve.

### Kingston

This small crag is located in the city of Kingston, approximately twenty minutes north of the Gunks. Once a quarry, the rock is not particularly pretty. But the routes are viciously difficult, making it a pumping experience. The small cliff boasts four 5.12ds, nine 5.13s, and one 5.14. One 5.11 exists as a warm-up. Not a bad purpose for an old quarry, if you ask me. Climbing at Kingston quarry is not a wilderness experience, so we will dispense with camping information.

There are many abandoned quarries in New York which may be of interest to the modern climber. You, however, will have to search for them yourself.

## New Mexico

### Cochiti Mesa

If you are into relentless pocket climbing, this is the place to find it. In fact, there are very few climbs at Cochiti that are *not* pocket climbs. The rock is volcanic tuff, and most of the routes use bolts as protection. There are many difficult routes, a few moderates, but very few easy ones. Camping is available anywhere near the area, but you will have to bring your own water, food, and so forth.

### Enchanted Tower

If you are passing through Socorro, New Mexico, you may want to make a small detour to the Enchanted Tower (or Box Canyon, located south of Magdalena). "The Tower" is composed of volcanic rock with excellent pocketed face climbing. Practically all of the faces overhang. Not too many routes exist, but their quality is certain to satisfy most climbers. To get there, head west out of Socorro on highway 60. Six miles after Datil, take a right (north) on a small dirt road. Follow this to the fork and turn left. You will soon see the tower off to your right (east). Have fun, and don't forget to tape up!

There is a lot of rock in New Mexico! Many new areas are being developed and are still "secret." If you are interested in obtaining information on newly developed areas, you will have to get to know the locals in Albuquerque or Santa Fe.

## North Carolina

### Moore's Wall

Moore's Wall is located in the Sauratown Range of North Carolina within the Hanging Rock State Park. The area is forty-five minutes north of Winston-Salem where you can get climbing information and supplies at Hills and Trails. The nearest store is Booths Shell (twenty minutes) where you can buy gas or food or eat at the restaurant. Other stores are available on highway 66 near Rural Hall. The climbing at Moore's Wall is on beautiful (and colorful) blue-gray quartzite. Many of the climbs fall into the 5.11 range of difficulty, but there are climbs for everyone from 5.5 to 5.14. There are bolt-protected climbs, but the majority of the routes take natural protection very well. The best seasons for climbing at Moore's Wall are spring and fall. Summers are typically hot and muggy, and bugs are abundant. The state park offers camping, showers, and toilets for a fee. Free camping may be available at the trailhead on locally owned land.

Several other climbing areas exist in North Carolina, but information is limited. You can probably find out more from the locals about Rumbling Bald, Looking Glass Mountain, and Stone Mountain, to name a few.

## Oklahoma

### *Quartz Mountain State Park*
Located in the southwestern corner of Oklahoma, Quartz is composed of granite and offers fine climbing. The climbing is traditional, with most of the routes being in the easy to moderate range. Routes require gear and, if bolt-protected, guts (the bolts are far apart). To get there, travel south from Carter after leaving Interstate Highway 40. Take the exit to Lugert (highway 44). After a few miles, you will reach the park entrance. Camping is available for a fee, and water is available at the camping area. Food and other items can be obtained in Lugert of Mangum.

### *Chandler Park*

This small bouldering area is located in Tulsa. The climbing is recommended if you're in this neck of the woods. The park is located in the bend of the Arkansas river.

## Oregon

### *Smith Rock*
Smith Rock was one of the first areas to be developed as a modern climbing area. Although it previously had been the location of numerous traditional climbs, the volcanic welded tuff rock faces were not explored with vigor until the early 1980's. Smith Rock has, at different times, been the location of the hardest route in America, which is not that amazing since it is also one of the most popular sport climbing areas and has been visited by some of the best climbers in the world. There are climbs, however, for everyone.

Smith Rock State Park is located approximately six miles north of Redmond, near the small town of Terrebonne. The park offers camping and facilities for a fee. Climbing information can be found in Terrebonne at Juniper Junction or Redpoint Climbers Supply.

## South Dakota

### Mount Rushmore

This climbing area, located in the Mount Rushmore National Memorial, offers outstanding climbing on pegmatite-laced granite spires and blades. The climbs are generally face routes, due to the lack of cracks, and are bolt-protected. You will find everything you need to survive in the nearby town of Keystone. If you need something that cannot be found in Keystone, it is another twenty-five miles to Rapid City. Climbing at Mount Rushmore is best in the fall, but you can experience fantastic days in the spring and summer also. The area offers a large number of climbs that are all easily accessible and varying in difficulty. Camping is available in the monument for a fee. Free camping can be found on nearby Forest Service land, but please be discrete.

## Tennessee

### Buzzard Point

This little-known area is the home of one of the country's hardest routes. At this time some 120 routes exist at Buzzard Point, and there are sure to be more. The high-quality white and orange sandstone offers excellent climbing on steep rock. Many of the routes are bolt-protected, and there are some outstanding cracks. The area offers a tranquil setting for those who do not wish to climb in a crowd. To get to Buzzard point, go north from Dayton, Tennessee, and take highway 30 west, just north of town. At the first traffic light, take a right and go up the mountain. Over the crest of the mountain, take the first right; this is Roger's Road. Follow the road along the power line, taking the first left you come to. Immediately take a right and follow this road through the field and into the woods as far as you can. Park your car in the woods. Camping is available at Buzzard point and in the parking lot. There are no facilities, so bring your own water and so on. You can climb here year 'round but the best seasons are spring and fall. It is possible to get good days in the winter and in summer also.

There are a few other climbing areas in this beautiful state. I'm sure the locals will share their treasure. Have fun, but don't venture too far into the woods!

## Texas

### *Hueco Tanks*

Hueco Tanks has long been the wintering area for some of the best climbers and boulderers in the United States. Its warm winters and overhanging routes offer superb training as well as climbs that are world class. The Hueco area is known as one of the finest bouldering areas in the world. We hope that it remains open for climbers in the future, although this possibility is threatened as of this writing due to squabbles over land ownership and vandalism that has taken place recently. The climbing area is located inside of Hueco Tanks State Historical park. It is subject to all state park regulations, and climbers should be aware of these restrictions. Camping is available in the park and just before the park at the legendary Quanset Hut.

### *Belton*

Near the small town of Belton, Texas, is an excellent cliff of limestone. There are several outstanding routes here if you are passing through central Texas. Belton is approximately 133 miles south of Dallas on Interstate Highway 35, and 69 miles north of Austin. Camping can be found a few miles east of Belton on Highway 36 at Mother Neff State Park. Food and gas are available in Belton or Temple. The winter months from October through April offer the best temperatures.

## Utah

### *American Fork*

The area's primarily bolt-protected routes start at a moderately high level of difficulty and extend to a few of the hardest routes in the country. The area is located above the beautiful Timpanogas Cave National Monument on the not-so-beautiful limestone. Although the rock is not so appealing visually, it does offer outstanding climbing on very steep rock. Many of the routes find their way out of the big limestone caves that have formed along the hillside. The climbing is on U.S. Forest Service land and is under their jurisdiction, so pay attention to local regulations. If you're interested in finding out more about park policies, information is available at the

Pleasant Grove Ranger Station or the visitor center at Timpanogas Cave. American Fork Canyon is located approximately twenty-five miles south of Salt Lake City. There are numerous places to get gas and food in the area. Camping is available in May through October at the Little Mill Campground, for a fee. Free camping is available above Table Rock Reservoir, located approximately three miles past Timpanogas Cave National Monument and two miles more up the North Fork. If you have questions about camping, check with the locals. Camping regulations are strictly enforced in the canyon. The best season for climbing in American Fork Canyon is April through October.

### Indian Creek

Modern rock climbing is not just bolt-protected face climbing. If you are up for the adventure and have a large rack of SLCDs and TCUs, you will find that climbing in Indian Creek is an existential experience. And if you have the heart and desire for adventure you will find that this canyon is only the beginning.

Indian creek is reached by driving 40 miles south from Moab on U.S. 191, then west on State Highway 211. Food and lodging can be found in Monticello. Camping is available near the climbing area in Indian Creek, but the area has seen some changes in camping policies due to the wishes of private land owners. Up-to-date information on the camping situation can be obtained in Moab at the Rim Cyclery (and climbing) Shop. The number of climbs in the area is increasing every year. Climbing is on Wingate sandstone, a hard and incredibly beautiful rock. The cracks are very parallel and accept camming devices exceptionally well. More information on routes can be found in Eric Bjornstad's guidebook, *Desert Rock*.

### Wall Street-Potash Road

This climbing area, just west of Moab, is an excellent diversion if you are passing through Moab. The climbs are located about two feet from the road that runs next to the Colorado river, between Moab and Potash. The climbs are on Navajo sandstone (a little softer than the wingate of Indian Creek) but are all well protected. The access is unbeatable. You can find everything you will need in the way of food, restaurants, and accommodations in Moab. Camping can be found in many areas surrounding

Moab. More information can be obtained at Rim Cyclery in Moab.

### Logan Canyon

This small canyon is located north of Logan, on highway 89. The climbing is on limestone (similar to that found in American Fork Canyon). There has been controversy as to whether or not climbing will be allowed to continue in the canyon, so if you plan to climb here, get some up-to-date information from the local climbing community.

Utah is well known for the large quantities of rock within its borders. Exploration of many areas has been minimal. If you are willing to get off the beaten track, there are literally thousands of gems to be found.

## West Virginia

### New River Gorge

"The New" is an extensive climbing area consisting of miles of compact Nuttall sandstone. There is so much rock that the new routes developed every year number in the hundreds. The gorge is located northeast of Fayetteville, West Virginia. A short fifteen-minute drive will get you to the nearest climbing; some of the other cliffs are a bit farther. The climbing here is world class, and you will find climbers from all over the country and even from around the world. There are climbs of all levels of difficulty. Camping information, food, gas, and such can be found in Fayetteville.

## Wisconsin

### Devils Lake State Park

This area is deep with history and has some of the hardest 5.11 routes you'll ever climb. Located approximately forty-five minutes northwest of Madison, near the small town of Baraboo, Devils Lake has a rich history filled with stories of legendary climbers and has at times had America's hardest routes. The rock is a very compact sandstone, with excellent crack climbing as well as a face climbing. Most routes are less than fifty feet long and require natural protection to lead. Many climbers prefer to top rope. There are several small sandstone crags near the main area that are being developed using modern methods of protection. To get to Devils Lake State Park from the south, take Interstate Highway 90 north from Madison. Shortly after crossing the Wisconsin River, turn west on highway 136 which will take you to the town of Baraboo. Gas, food, and entertainment can be found in Baraboo. Leave Baraboo heading south, and follow the signs to Devils Lake State Park. Camping and water are available in the park.

## Wyoming

### Fremont Canyon

If you are looking for a nice change of pace and some excellent crack climbing, as well as outstanding face climbing, Fremont Canyon is a primo choice. The canyon is located south of Casper near the Pathfinder Reserve. To get to Fremont Canyon, take highway 220 south from Casper for approximately eighteen miles. Turn left at the sign for the Alcova Dam. This junction also has the nearest stores, food, and gas. Follow this dirt road to the turn off to Pathfinder Dam and Reserve. You will soon come to an old bridge. Hey! Look down, you're there! A good camping area is located about a quarter of a mile past the bridge on a dirt road that leads off to the left. There are many routes in the canyon, and I would suggest getting a guide so you won't get yourself "in too deep." Once you rappel in, you have to climb out. There are other nice routes farther south near the base of the Pathfinder Dam.

### Wild Iris

This once "secret" crag has become extremely popular to many modern climbers. Just forty-five minutes south of Lander, Wild Iris is just the tip of the iceberg of Wyoming dolomite. Composed of compact white dolomite limestone, many of the sections of Wild Iris will remind you of France's Buoux. There are well over a hundred routes, with much more potential. The area is secluded, beautiful, and offers some of the finest climbing in the country. Routes rate from 5.9 to 5.14, and many more are sure to be discovered. The best weather conditions are spring through fall. Occasionally the winter months give in, producing fine days. Camping is free nearby. There are no facilities in the area, so come prepared or you'll have to drive back to Lander to stock up.

### Sinks Canyon

Sinks Canyon offers extensive climbing. There are three layers of rock, the lowermost a fine layer of sandstone offering outstanding moderate climbing in cracks and on faces. The mid-layer is dolomite and is the location of the area's highest use and development. There are nearly a hundred routes in the dolomite section of the canyon, and there are surely going to be more. The upper layer of rock is granite where many excellent routes have been established. If you are looking to experience many varieties of rock while climbing in one general location, Sinks Canyon can't be beat! Located a couple of miles south of Lander on highway 131, the climbing area is near town. Food and gas are easily accessible. The climbing season is generally year 'round, spring and fall being the best. Winter can be surprisingly mild (if the conditions are mild, it is possible to get many good climbing days in even in December and January). Camping is available nearby. A pay area offers some facilities, and a free camping area without facilities can be found farther up the canyon. For more information on climbing in the Lander area, drop into the Wild Iris Climbing Shop in Lander.

### Vedauwoo (pronounced vee da voo)

High-altitude prairie surrounds this beautiful climbing area. Vedauwoo is best known for its notorious off-width cracks and the rough, painful texture of the granite. Don't let this scare you away. Very fine routes have been established here. Located on Interstate Highway 80 between Laramie and Cheyenne, Vedauwoo is easily accessible. There are nice camping areas available and water and rest rooms for a modest fee. Most of the routes were put up in traditional style, so you will need a rack of gear to climb these. There are a few excellent bolt-protected routes easy to get to and very enjoyable. The best seasons for climbing at Vedauwoo are spring, summer, and fall.

Wyoming has so much rock that you could be overwhelmed by the potential number of climbs that remain to be done. If you are interested in the future, this is one place to be.

This by no means locates all of the climbing areas in the United States. For more information on climbing and climbing areas, visit your local bookstore, climbing shop, or library. Have fun, travel widely and treat every area as if it were your own.

# Appendix

Figure A-1

**Figure A-2** A few of our favorite east coast climbing areas.

**Figure A-3**   A few of our favorite mid-west climbing areas.

**Figure A-4** A few of our favorite west coast climbing areas.

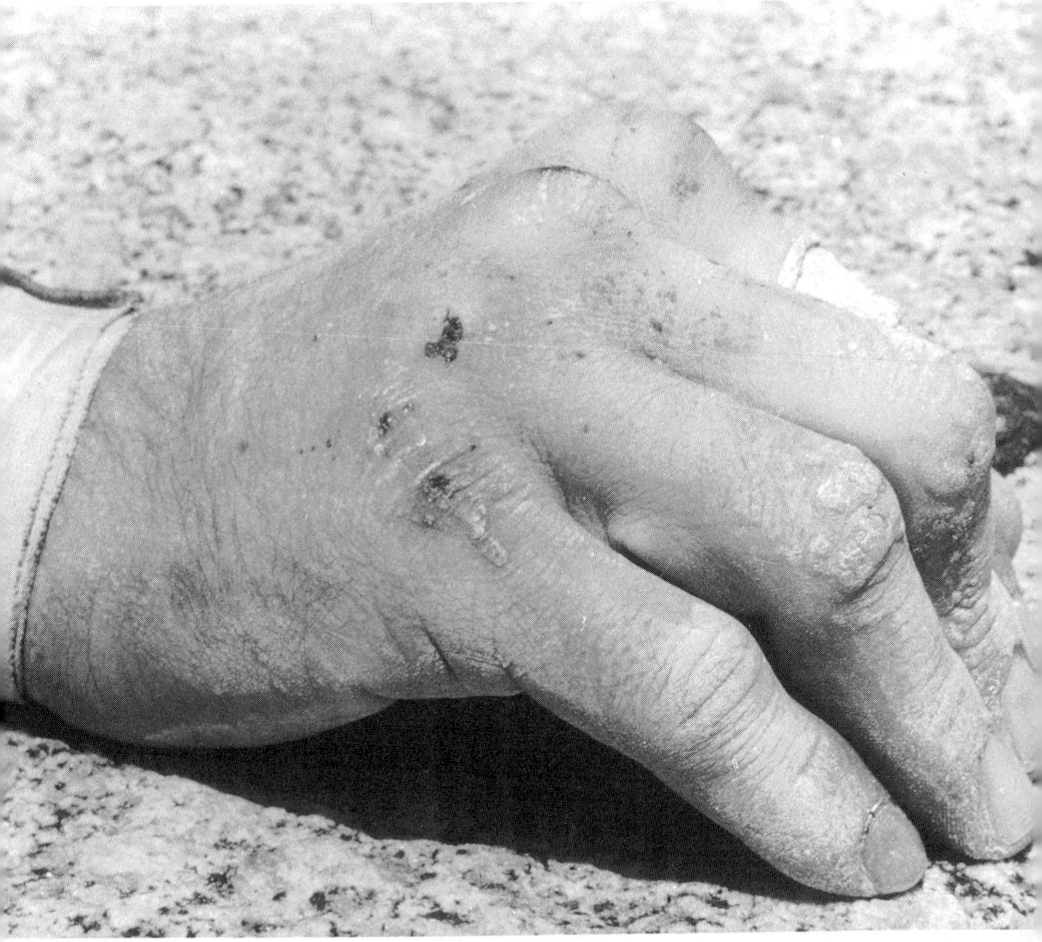

# GLOSSARY

**Advanced Top Rope:** A top rope set up that requires technical knowledge of knots, with possible use of more than one anchor point or more than one rope.

**Aerobics:** Conditioning of the cardiopulmonary system by means of vigorous exercise that oxygenates the muscle and tissue of the body.

**Aid Climbing:** Climbing technique that requires the direct use of gear to make progress up the rock.

**Anchors, Belay:** The anchors that are used at a belay.

**Anchors, Protection:** The anchors placed along the way that are used to protect the climber.

**Arete:** A ridge or corner of rock.

**Artificial Hold:** Plastic, fiberglass, or other materials that are applied to a surface for the purpose of climbing.

**Back Stepping:** Technique using the outside edge of the foot on a hold which is under or behind you while climbing.

141

**Back Up Knot:** A knot tied behind or after a main knot to prevent the main knot from untying. Also called a "safety."

**Ball Nut™:** A small nut with expanding surfaces. Designed to fit into exceptionally small cracks.

**Belay Anchor:** The anchor or anchors placed or permanently fixed at a belay.

**Belay device:** Any mechanical device used for belaying.

**Belay Exchange:** When the leader passes the gear and leading responsibility to the other climber on the team. Requires organization of equipment and mental alertness on the part of both climbers.

**Belay Position:** A stance or position assumed by the belayer so that he is ready and braced (and anchored) in the event of a fall by the leader.

**Belay Station:** A permanent or regularly used belay position on a route.

**Belayer:** The person who is managing the rope and protecting the climber with it.

**Belaying:** The act of managing a climbing rope which is attached to a climber and safeguarding the climber.

**Beta:** A verbal description of moves or technical information involved in climbing a particular route.

**Big Wall Climbing:** Climbing large walls. Big wall climbs often require aid climbing technique and many days of climbing before the summit can be reached. However, using modern methods and equipment, the amount of time that was once required for many big wall routes has been greatly reduced.

**Bight, Rope:** Any knot that is tied in the middle of a length of rope.

**Biner Saver:** Using a large, locking carabiner in place of a quick draw saves wear on lightweight carabiners.

**Board Last:** A method of shoe construction. The method most commonly used in the construction of the average street shoe.

**Bolt:** Concrete bolts are used in climbing as permanent anchors on many climbs. They are used for belay anchors as well as for protection anchors on aid and free climbs. Some bolts are made specifically for climbing protection. These types of bolts are the best choice for use as permanent anchors on rock climbs.

**Bomber:** A very secure anchor or hold is often referred to as being "Bomber."

**Bouldering:** Climbing on boulders close to the ground. Bouldering can be done with or without a rope and is a great way to train for difficult longer routes. The most difficult single moves in climbing are found in bouldering. It is considered a sport in itself. Climbing on buildings (similar to bouldering) is called buildering.

**Bowline:** The traditional knot used by climbers to be tied around the waist or to a swami-belt or harness loop. Not as common now due to harness technology and fads.

**Bowline on a Bight:** A bowline knot that is tied in the middle of a length of rope.

**Bowline on a Coil:**

**Caffeine:** a bitter alkaloid, usually obtained from coffee or tea. Generally used as a stimulant.

**Camelot™:** A spring-loaded camming device designed and manufactured by Black Diamond Equipment.

**Carabiner:** An aluminum ring with a spring-loaded gate. Used to connect the climber's equipment and protection to a rope. Carabiners come in a large variety of shapes and sizes.

**Chalk Bag:** The small bag used to carry chalk (and attached to the climber).

**Chalk:** Carbonate of Magnesium. Carried in a chalk bag on the climber's waist. Chalk is used to aid in neutralizing the moisture in the fingers and hands. It also acts as a protective agent to holds.

**Cheater Stick:** Any stick or extension device that aids in attaching a carabiner of placing protection about a climber's head.

**Chronic:** Used as noun (colloquially) to refer to an injury that lasts a long time or recurs.

**Clean Climbing:** The use of protection that does not damage the rock.

**Clean Protection:** A piece of protection that will not harm the rock.

**Cleaning (a pitch):** The act of removing equipment from a pitch.

**Cleaning (a route):** The act of removing dirt or loose rock from a climb.

**Climbing Wall:** An artificial (or man-made) climbing surface.

**Clip:** The act of clipping a rope into a quick draw (or clipping a carabiner to a point of protection).

**Clove Hitch:** A simple knot often used at belays because of its ease of adjustment.

**Crack Climbing:** Ascending any crack in the rock, using wedge techniques with hands or body.

**Crag Pack:** A small backpack, just large enough to hold climbing gear and extra food & clothing.

**Crag:** A small cliff.

**Crimpers:** A term used by climbers to describe small edges used as hand holds.

**Cromolybdenum:** A type of metal commonly used in manufacturing climbing pitons. It is hard but not brittle.

**Crux:** a difficult move. The most difficult sections of a climb are often referred to as crux sections.

**Dead Point:** A dynamic yet controlled throw to a hold.

**Diet:** Refers to the food and liquid consumed daily.

**Dome:** Granite monoliths that were fully or partially exposed to glaciers and thus smoothed to a dome-like appearance. Any rock that looks like a dome.

**Double Bowline Knot:** A bowline knot created using two loops instead of the one.

**Double Clipping:** When the lead rope is passed through both the carabiners of a quick draw.

**Dynamic Move:** A fully dynamic move usually entails leaving the rock completely in order to reach the desired hold. A lunge for a hold or swing move would also be considered dynamic.

**Dynamic Rope:** A Kernmantle rope that stretches in order to absorb the force of a fall.

**Dyno:** (see Dynamic Move.)

**Edge:** A sharp protrusion of rock or small foothold.

**Edging:** The act of standing on an edge of rock with the edge of the foot.

**End Of Pitch:** A pitch can mean a couple of things, but it is basically a measurement. A pitch can be short in length or as long as the length of a rope. The end of a pitch is therefore the position of a belay or, in the case of a short route, the end of the climb.

**Extension,Rope:**  A piece of rope that is used to extend an anchor.

**Face Climbing:**  Climbing a rock wall that has no (or few) cracks.

**Fall:**  When your are not touching the rock any more, you are generally taking a fall.

**Falling:**  What happens when you let go.

**Figure Eight Descending Device:** A rappel belay device that is shaped like an eight.

**Figure Eight Knot:**  The popular knot for tying the rope to one's harness. This is a must know knot! It can be tied at the end of a rope or on a bight.

**Figure Four:**  An advanced climbing move where the climber throws one leg over a wrist or arm that is holding onto a hold. Using the leg to push the body higher, the climber is then able to reach holds that would not be reachable otherwise.

**Finger Board:**  A board with a variety of holds on it enabling the climber to strengthen hands, back, and arms. Used for pull-ups and other exercises.

**Finger Jam:**  A hold using fingers jammed in a crack.

**Fist Jam:**  Wedging a fist in a crack for a hold.

**Fixed Anchor:**  Anchors such as bolts or pitons that are left in place.

**Fixed Pin:**  Pitons that are left at belay stations or on a pitch are referred to as fixed pitons.  These are left in place to eliminate the rock damage of repeated placements or are too well placed to remove.

**Flagging:** A climbing technique whereby one foot is used behind the other to keep the body in balance.

**Flash, lead:** When a climber leads a route with prior knowledge of the route but does not fall.

**Flash, Top Rope:** When a climber is successful at top roping a route, without falling but has prior knowledge of the route's problems.

**Food Bars:** Condensed foods with concentrated ingredients for quick energy.

**Footwork:** The use of the feet or shoes while climbing.

**Free Climbing:** The term used to describe a style of climbing where the climber is not directly using equipment to ascend. When free climbing, the climber uses physical strength, technique, footwork, etc. to ascend the rock. Equipment is used by the climber as a backup in the event of a fall or to secure a belay.

**Free Weight Training:** Free weight training involves the use of a bar, bars, or dumbbells (hand weights) and steel (or plastic) weights in conjunction with a variety of exercises for specific muscles or muscle groups.

**Friction Slab Smearing:** Using the friction created between the weight of the climber and the climber's shoes to ascend a smooth piece of rock.

**Friend™:** A spring-loaded camming device manufactured by Wild Country.

**Gear Loop:** A loop of plastic perlon, or webbing that is attached to the waist belt of a harness. Used to carry climbing equipment.

**Grade:** Classifications given to routes that denote the level of difficulty one may encounter.

**Grapevine Knot:**  A climbing knot used to tie two pieces of rope together.

**GriGri:**  A mechanical belay device manufactured by Petzl. An active camming system which locks in the event of a fall.

**Hand Jam:**  By forcing the hand into a wide position, the friction between the hand and the sides of the crack allow it to be used as a hold. Using various types of jams allows the climber to make progress up a crack.

**Hanger, Bolt:**  Hangers are attached to bolts. The climber's quick draw is attached to the hanger.

**Harness:**  Climbing harnesses are constructed of various types of webbing (fitting around the legs and waist) and are designed to distribute the force generated on the climber's body in the event of a fall.

**Heel Hooking:**  A climbing technique using the heel of the foot on a hold.

**Hexentric™:**  An offset nut that is shaped in the form of a hexentric. A shape that works well in nearly parallel cracks.

**Home Gyms:**  Refers to artificial climbing structures built inside a home.

**Hooking:**  An aid climbing technique where a metal hook or hooks of different shapes and sizes are used on flakes in order to ascend a rock face.

**Horn:**  A rock feature that protrudes from the surface like a horn.

**Hueco:**  A large pocket in rock formed by water or wind.

**Improved Prusik:**  A knot used in conjunction with a carabiner which enables the climber to ascend a rope.

**Jamming:** The technique a climber uses to climb cracks.

Some part of the climber's body is inserted into the crack and twisted, widened, or manipulated in order for the climber to make progress up the crack. Requires good technique (practice) to avoid injury.

**Kernmantle:** A method of rope construction. Consists of an outer section (the mantle) and an inner section (the core).

**Leading:** Whenever one is climbing without protection from above, one is leading. A climber can lead a route using aid or free climbing protection methods in unison with a belay from a partner below.

**Ledge:** An outcrop of rock suitable to stand or sit on.

**Logistics:** The requirements of planning, preparing for, organizing, and approaching a climb.

**Lineback:** Leaning out (pulling) on the arms in opposition to the feet.

**Lowering:** Being lowered to the ground by a belayer.

**Lunge:** A somewhat uncontrolled dynamic move. (see dynamic)

**Mental Training:** Mental preparation often consists of training, discipline, visualization, and forms of meditation.

**Mono Doigt (One finger):** A mono would indicate that only one finger can be used in or on a hold.

**Mountaineering:** Climbing mountains. Mountaineering requires the use of snow and ice climbing skills as well as rock climbing experience.

**Multi-Pitch Route:** A climb more than one pitch long.

**Nail Drive Bolt:** A bolt that consists of a sleeve and a nail. The nail is driven into the sleeve, forcing it outward and tight in the hole.

**Nubbin:** A small pebble attached to a face of rock.

**Nut:** A piece of clean climbing equipment. Called "nuts" because actual machine nuts were once used as clean climbing protection.

**Nut Tool:** A tool used to aid in the removal of nuts that have become stuck.

**Nutrients:** Elements that provide nourishment or nutriment.

**On-sight:** When a climb is done without any prior knowledge, it is called an on-sight ascent.

**Overhang:** Overhangs or "roofs," as they are often called, are steep sections of rock that can be difficult to climb. Some overhangs are completely horizontal.

**Permanent Anchor:** An anchor which is left in place or permanently attached to the rock.

**Pitons:** Metal spikes that are hammered into cracks for use as aid or protection while climbing rock. Pitons come in various sizes and shapes for use in cracks ranging from one sixteenth of an inch (Rurps and Bird Beaks) to six inches (bongs).

**Placement:** The quality of a piece of protection, or simply the place where a piece of protection is set.

**Plastic:** Climbing on artificial holds and walls is often referred to as climbing plastic.

**Pockets:** Refers to holes in rock which are used as holds.

**Pre clip:** When protection is in place and the rope is attached to runners or quick draws prior to climbing.

**Previewing:** When one rappels down a route to study, feel, and look at the available holds prior to an ascent.

**Protection:** Refers to equipment used to provide safety for a climber.

**Proteins:** A group of nitrogenous organic compounds of high molecular weight that occur in all living cells and that are required for all life processes in animals and plants.

**Pumped:** The filling of the blood vessels in a appendage due to extreme physical exertion. A muscularly tired condition after hard climbing.

**Quick Draw:** A sewn or tied piece of nylon webbing that connects two carabiners.

**Rand:** The piece of rubber in a climbing shoe that wraps around the sole and lower part of the shoe.

**Rappelling:** Descending by sliding down a rope.

**Rating:** An approximate numerical classification given to a climb to indicate the difficulty of the climb. Based on the OPINION of the first ascent team, a rating can be updated or adjusted by the ascents of others after the first ascent.

**Recover:** A period of rest after physical exertion.

**Red Point:** A red point can only be claimed if the climber climbs the route from the ground to the anchors with no falls.

**Rehearsing:** Practicing the moves on a climb.

**Rest:** A point or position on a climb where one can rest.

**Rock Gym:** An indoor climbing gym. Designed with the esoteric training needs of the modern climber in mind.

**Roof:** A horizontal section of rock.

**Rope Bag:** A bag or pack designed to carry and protect a climbing rope (without having to coil the rope).

**Rope Drag:**  Friction, commonly generated by contact with rock or by the rope running in various directions through protection.

**Rope Stretch:**  The amount of stretch in a dynamic climbing rope.

**RP:**  A small version of a nut.  The wedge portion of a RP is made of brass, and the cable is soldered into the wedge- allowing the nut to be made in very small sizes.  Small nuts similar to the RP are now being made of steel also.

**Runner:**  Runners (sling webbing or cord) are designed to be extensions for pieces of protection. They allow the rope to run freely, thus reducing the amount of rope drag.  Runners are also used for a variety of purposes, from belay anchor extensions to lassos for protection on rock horns or flakes.

**Runout:**  Any section of a climb where the leader is forced to climb high and dangerously above protection.

**Self Drive Bolt:**  A self drive bolt has teeth on one end and a threaded hole on the other end.  The bolt is attached to a driver handle and used as a drill.  When the hole is drilled, the handle is removed.  A wedge is inserted into the drill end, a hanger and bolt attached to the other end, and then the bolt is driven into the hole.

**SLCD (Spring-Loaded Camming Device):**  Examples of SLCDs are Friends, Camelots, and TCUs.  There are many brands of SLCDs available. SLCDs are constructed of three to four cams which are spring-loaded to open.  A trigger allows the cams to compress in size, thus allowing the protection to be placed in the crack.  Upon releasing the trigger, the cams open (expand), securing the protection within the crack.

**Slip Last:**  A type of shoe construction consisting of two parts to the upper.  When sewn together, the "upper" forms a sock like fit.

**Smearing:**  When a rock shoe is pressed against a surface, creating friction.

**Solo:** Climbing alone. Aid soloists generally use a rope, free soloists do not.

**Sport Climbing:** Indoor climbing in a controlled atmosphere, for fun or competition. A term used by some to describe modern rock climbing on bolt-protected routes.

**Spot:** A person who stands below and acts as a safety net to protect a climber who is close to the ground.

**Spring/Boing:** A technique where a free-hanging climber (after a fall) hoists his body in short bursts to let the belayer pull in rope, in an effort to regain contact with the rock.

**Stance:** A body position. Generally refers to a belay or rest position.

**Static Belay:** A belay where the belayer lets no rope out at all.

**Static Move:** A controlled move from one hold to another, where the climber maintains contact with the rock at one point at least. A slow one-arm pullup could be called a static move, but usually there are two points of contact.

**Static Rope:** A rope that does not stretch.

**Stemming:** A spread-eagle body position where force is applied from a central position onto holds or planes of rock to either side of the body.

**Sticht Plate:** A simple belay device that relies on friction. Sticht plates have no moving parts and are very light.

**Stopper™:** A nut manufactured by Black Diamond Equipment. Originally designed by Tom Frost and Yvon Chouinard, Stoppers have evolved to become quite versatile and an essential part of any climber's equipment arsenal.

**Stretching:** Warming and stretching the muscles by doing slow, deliberate, almost yoga like exercises. Stretching should be included in every climber's training routine.

**Style:** The method used to achieve an ascent.

**Supertape:** A strong but light type of nylon webbing.

**Supplements:** Additional vitamins or other nutrients. Often used by athletes who train hard, depleting their natural intake of these elements.

**Taping:** Protection the parts of the body that are prone to injury with athletic tape, and also the hands for painful cracks.

**TCU (Three Cam Unit):** A small spring-loaded camming device for use in small, narrow, or shallow cracks.

**Top Rope:** Having a rope from above. Top roping does not require the use of equipment for protection while climbing, although some equipment may be need as an anchor to set up a top rope.

**Training:** Physical and mental exercises that are specifically designed to improve your performance on a given sport or endeavor.

**Tuffskin:** A spray that improves the stickiness of tape, thus allowing it to attach to your skin more securely.

**Tying in:** The attachment of rope to the climber's harness. Undercling: A kind of lieback, with the palms up (under a hold).

**Varnish:** A hard coating of minerals that forms on the surface of rock.

**Visualization:** A method of training the mind which allows the climber to flow through the moves of a climb mentally and to "visualize" success.

**Warm up:** The act of warming muscles to prevent injury.

**Weight Machines:** Training machines that allow you to exercise a specific muscle or muscle group-generally with more control than free weights.

**Work Out:** A training session.

**Working:** Practicing the moves on a climb before doing them. Or trying to figure out the moves on a new route.

**X Position:** A body position which allows the climber to rest somewhat.

# INDEX

**Climbing Adventures**
**a climber's passion**
**by Jim Bridwell with Keith Peall**
$16.50 paperback • $21.50 Canada
216 pages • 6x9 inches • illustration • 16
stories   EAN code • ISBN 0-934802-22-X
Climbing Adventures, Never so outrageous
includes sixteen accounts of ascents involving
travel to countries world wide during period
of time and place in which little has been
written. The book is jammed with humorous
interludes into the lives and lifestyles of
climbers and mountaineers  This is Jim
Bridwell's first feature book.

Jim Bridwell is more than an extreme climber.
He is a character. A wild man, who finally
tells us about his wild life.
          –Reinhold Messner
          World renowned author and climber

**CLIMBING BIG WALLS**
**by Mike Strassman**
$9.99 paperback • $11.99 Canada
128 pages • 6x9 inches • illustrations • index
EAN code • ISBN 0-934802-59-9
This is a technical book about big wall
climbing features first rate personnel like
Mike Strassman, Jim Bridwell, Steve
Grossman, Randy Leavitt, John Middendorf,
and Steve Schnieder.

"Climbing Big Walls is long overdue and
much-needed instructional manual that
removes the mystery from one of the most
challenging and committing branches of the
climbing game ... Although hard-learned
lessons are useful because they aren't soon
repeated, nobody wants to experiment cold
with expando-flake nailing halfway up an A5
nightmare like Scorched Earth. Today, thanks
to Climbing Big Walls, nobody has to. "
—CLIMBING MAGAZINE